THE COMPLETE GUIDE TO
KENTUCKY STATE PARKS

THE COMPLETE GUIDE TO
KENTUCKY STATE PARKS

WRITTEN BY **Susan Reigler**

PHOTOGRAPHY BY **Pam Spaulding**

The University Press of Kentucky

Copyright © 2009 by The University Press of Kentucky
Scholarly publisher for the Commonwealth,
serving Bellarmine University, Berea College, Centre
College of Kentucky, Eastern Kentucky University,
The Filson Historical Society, Georgetown College,
Kentucky Historical Society, Kentucky State University,
Morehead State University, Murray State University,
Northern Kentucky University, Transylvania University,
University of Kentucky, University of Louisville,
and Western Kentucky University.

Editorial and Sales Offices: The University Press of Kentucky
663 South Limestone Street, Lexington, Kentucky 40508-4008
www.kentuckypress.com

13 12 11 10 09   5 4 3 2 1

Library of Congress Cataloging-in-Publication Data
Reigler, Susan.
The complete guide to Kentucky state parks /
written by Susan Reigler ; photography by Pam Spaulding.
    p. cm.
Includes index.
ISBN 978-0-8131-9208-6 (pbk. : alk. paper)
1. Parks—Kentucky—Guidebooks. 2. Kentucky—Guidebooks.
I. Spaulding, Pam. II. Title.
F449.3.R45 2009
917.69'0444—dc22   2008037331

∞ This book is printed on acid-free paper meeting
the requirements of the American National Standard
for Permanence in Paper for Printed Library Materials.
Manufactured in China.

AAUP Member of the Association of
American University Presses

Frontispiece: Clinchfield Overlook at Breaks State Park.
Design: Julie Allred, BW&A Books, Inc., Durham, NC

To Joanna, Gervase, and Winston,
devotees of the license plate game

CONTENTS

BUCKSKIN-CLAD LONG HUNTERS (one who hunts for weeks or months at a time), dense woodlands that shelter bears, roaming herds of elk and bison, and wetlands where bald eagles perch in overhanging branches are all sights that would have been familiar to Kentucky's most famous early citizen, Daniel Boone.

Were Boone to return to the state today, he would find all these sights preserved and protected in Kentucky's state parks. Even his eponymous settlement, Fort Boonesborough, is still around, though rebuilt and moved a bit from its original site. And he might be tempted to take up golf or sailing, have a swim in an Olympic-size pool, or spend a warm summer evening outdoors enjoying a musical or a concert. The parks offer all these things, too.

Thanks to the foresight of Kentucky's citizens in the early part of the last century, the state's General Assembly created the State Parks Commission in 1924 and so began the preservation of unique scenic areas and important historic sites. It started with 4 parks. Today there are 52 if you include Pine Mountain Trail State Park, a 120-mile backcountry hiking trail under development, or 53 if you count the interstate park shared with Virginia. Together they constitute what has to be the best public "backyard" in the country.

They encompass almost 50,000 acres and include or are situated on the shores of almost 350,000 acres of lakes. They provide a combination of natural and historic preservation and recreation, from tiny Isaac Shelby Cemetery State Historic Site near Danville (only 0.25 acre, the resting place of the state's first governor) to Breaks Interstate Park (4,600 acres of rugged, forested mountain terrain covering parts of both Kentucky and Virginia through which the Russell Fork River has carved a five-mile-long, 1,600-foot-deep canyon). Hikers and backpackers will find 250 miles of trails to explore. Included in the system are many wonderful indoor assets, too, from graceful antebellum mansions to log meetinghouses. Kentucky classifies its parks in three categories.

Resort parks, of which there are 17 (more than in any other state), have lodges with dining rooms and cottages to accommodate visitors who go to them to enjoy their natural settings. Many of these parks, including Cumberland Falls State Resort Park and Pennyrile Forest State Resort Park, contain architecturally and historically significant buildings, such as lodges and cottages constructed in the 1930s by the Works Progress Administration and Civilian Conservation Corps.

The 24 recreational parks do not have lodges, though many have campsites and one has cottages. They offer facilities for hiking, birding, fishing, boating, golf, and other outdoor activities. Like many resort parks, several recreational parks are on land associated with historic events, such as Fort Boonesborough State Park and My Old Kentucky Home State Park.

Historic sites (11 in all) commemorate events that occurred over many centuries, from Wickcliffe Mounds State Historic Site, where Mississippian mound builders lived from about 1100 to 1350, to Perryville Battlefield State Historic Site, where the state's largest Civil War battle took place in 1862. Colorful figures from Kentucky's past include John James Audubon, Abraham Lincoln, Jenny Wiley, and Stephen Foster, and each, like Daniel Boone, has parks associated with his or her time in the state.

The parks are extremely popular. According to the Kentucky Department of Parks, some 7 million visitors per year, including nature lovers, history buffs, sports enthusiasts, and people simply looking for an affordable weekend getaway, visit the properties in the system.

This book was written to help you explore the parks, including the many in which you can literally follow in Daniel Boone's footsteps. What I have tried to do in these pages is give you an armchair traveler description of what being in each park is like. Some entries describe specific events, while others give more general descriptions. Pam Spaulding's beautiful photos give you a sense of each place, too. Perhaps it should be mentioned that all efforts, whether oral or written, were made to ensure the human subjects in the photographs were aware that their likeness would be included in this book. Anyone believing he or she was not asked may contact the publisher.

The sections of the book are arranged geographically, using the regions designated by the Kentucky Department of Parks—north central, south central, eastern, and western. Within each region, the parks are listed alphabetically.

Also included in each park's listing is a description of facilities. I have not noted specific fees or hours because these are subject to change. Park phone numbers and Web sites are included so you can check on the most recent details. Some attractions within parks charge admission, but unlike in many other states, you can drive or walk around the grounds of any Kentucky state park free of charge. Since the meals I had in lodge restaurants were of decidedly mixed quality, and nothing is more changeable than a restaurant kitchen, I have not attempted to critique park menus.

The home page of the Kentucky state parks is http://www.parks.ky.gov/. In addition to links to each park's page with current rates and fees, this site has information about special system-wide deals, including golf packages and adventure and history trails. From this site, you can order maps and purchase gift cards that can be used throughout the system.

Assume that, if you are going to engage in fishing or hunting where permitted, you will need to purchase the appropriate license. Check out the Kentucky Department of Fish and Wildlife Resources at http://www.fw.ky.gov/ for season and licensing information.

The state parks system has a couple of important partners in its efforts to preserve the state's natural assets and provide great places for people to relax. One is the Kentucky State Nature Preserves Commission, which oversees the protection of rare and endangered species within the boundaries of several parks. These are noted in the text. For details, go to http://www.naturepreserves.ky.gov/.

The other partner is the U.S. Army Corps of Engineers. Colonel Boone would be very surprised to find today's Kentucky dotted with lakes. When he and the other pioneers came through the Cumberland Gap and made their way to the central part of what would become the 15th state, the landscape was laced with a network of streams and rivers. In the 20th century, the Army Corps of Engineers and the Tennessee Valley Authority dammed many of these for flood control. The resulting lakes provided a bounty of new recreational opportunities, and state parks were created on land leased to Kentucky by the Army Corps of Engineers. That is why you will find so many parks situated on lakes.

In addition to the 52 officially designated Kentucky state parks, three additional facilities, which are not on the state parks Web site, are included. They are Breaks Interstate Park (which is co-owned and operated with Virginia), Falls of the Ohio State Park (in Indiana, directly across the Ohio River from Louisville), and Kentucky Horse Park (state owned, so it honors the parks system's gift card).

You will also find tips for further exploration at the end of each park entry. They may be about a nearby attraction, a useful reference for more park information, or a good place to stay or eat if the park does not have a lodge. Basic park history is included in each entry, but visit the Web site for details I could not include because of space constraints.

Finally, having spent a busy and fascinating year traveling to each park, I have some suggestions for your visits. Field guides and binoculars will be indispensable to nature lovers. If you are staying in a cottage (all of which have kitchens) and are self-catering, bring paper towels. Keep in mind that no alcohol is served in lodge restaurants. If you bring your own to a campsite or cottage, be discreet. If you want a park all to yourself, visit during the week after a big holiday weekend. The first week in June (after Memorial Day) and the week after the Fourth of July are quiet in the parks. Interested in fall color? Book accommodations for the mountain parks as much as a year in advance. The lodges have Wi-Fi for your laptop, but the signals are unpredictable.

What is predictable is that Kentucky's state parks offer special pleasures for every visitor. I hope this book helps you plan trips as memorable as mine were. I can hardly wait to go back!

NORTH CENTRAL KENTUCKY PARKS

OHIO

INDIANA

0 10 20
Miles

Big Bone Lick State Park

General Butler State Resort Park

Kincaid Lake State Park

Blue Licks Battlefield State Resort Park

E. P. "Tom" Sawyer State Park

Taylorsville Lake State Park

My Old Kentucky Home State Park

Waveland State Historic Site

Boone Station State Historic Site

Old Fort Harrod State Park

White Hall State Historic Site

Fort Boonesborough State Park

Lincoln Homestead State Park

Constitution Square State Historic Site

Perryville Battlefield State Historic Site

Isaac Shelby Cemetery State Historic Site

Rough River Dam State Resort Park

William Whitley House State Historic Site

Nolin Lake State Park

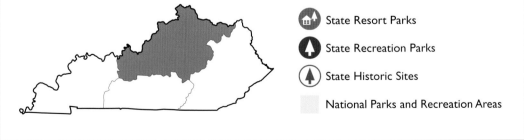

State Resort Parks

State Recreation Parks

State Historic Sites

National Parks and Recreation Areas

1

NORTH CENTRAL STATE PARKS

- • Year-round
- ○ Seasonal

		Park Acres	Lake Acres	Lodge and Dining Room	Cottages	Campground	✈ : Airport; ▲ : Air Camp
RESORT PARKS							
Blue Licks Battlefield	Carlisle	580		•	•	○	
General Butler	Carrollton	791	30	•	•	•	
Rough River Dam	Falls of Rough	637	4,860	•	•	•	✈▲
RECREATIONAL PARKS							
Big Bone Lick	Union	525	7.5			•	
E. P. "Tom" Sawyer	Louisville	513					
Fort Boonesborough	Richmond	153				•	
Kincaid Lake	Falmouth	919	183			○	
Lincoln Homestead	Springfield	230	41				
My Old Kentucky Home	Bardstown	290				○	
Nolin Lake	Bee Spring	333	5,795			○	
Old Fort Harrod	Harrodsburg	32					
Taylorsville Lake	Taylorsville	2,560	3,050			○	
HISTORIC SITES							
Boone Station	Lexington	46					
Constitution Square	Danville	3					
Isaac Shelby Cemetery	Junction City	0.25					
Perryville Battlefield	Perryville	669					
Waveland	Lexington	14					
White Hall	Richmond	13					
William Whitley House	Stanford	40					

Golf (18-Hole, 9-Hole, or D. Disc Course)	Marina (L: Boat Launch Only)	Rental Boats	Swimming (P: Outdoor Pool, I: Indoor Pool, S: Slide, B: Beach)	Trails (Miles)	Riding Stables (U: Equestrian Trails)	Mountain Biking	Tennis Courts	Miniature Golf	Playgrounds	Picnic Area	Museum or Nature Center	Recreation/Interpretation Program
	L		P	5				○	●	●	●	●
9		○	P	6		●	●	○	●	●	●	●
P3	○	○	P/B	1			●	○	●	●		●
			P	3.5			●	○	●	●	●	○
			P	2.25			●		●	●		●
	L		P/S	0.25				○	●	●	○	○
9	○	○	P	2.5			●	○	●	●		○
18			P						●	●	○	○
18							●		●	●	●	●
	L		B	1.6					●	●		
									●	●	●	●
	○	○		16	U	●			●	●		
				1						●		
										●	●	●
										●		
				7					●	●	●	●
				0.25					●	●	●	●
				0.1						●	○	○
				1					●	●	○	○

BIG BONE LICK STATE PARK

3380 Beaver Union Road
Union, KY 41091-9627
(859) 384-3522
http://www.parks.ky.gov/findparks/recparks/bb/
525 acres; 7.5 lake acres

WHEN EUROPEAN EXPLORERS ventured down the Ohio River in the 18th century, they followed a wide buffalo trace from the river's south bank and discovered a 10-acre bog dotted with mineral springs. Large game animals, including bison, deer, and elk, were attracted to the salty, sulfurous water. This made the swamp a perfect hunting ground for the area's American Indians, and so it seemed perfectly natural, too, to find scores of large bones mired in quivering mud. Indeed, the "jelly ground," as the explorers called it, often trapped unwary beasts coming to the springs to drink. But these were no mere bison bones. Bison do not have tusks.

Monstrous fossilized bones, including fist-size teeth, leg bones the explorers used as tent poles, and elephantine tusks from which ivory was extracted, were among the thousands of remains that gave the site its name—Big Bone Lick. The fossils caused quite a stir, since it was obvious that the animals to which they had belonged were no longer around. In the 18th century, any concept that creation was changeable, that God had made mistakes and animals became extinct, was not tenable. Indeed it was considered blasphemous.

Tons of fossil bones were shipped to centers of natural history scholarship such as Philadelphia, London, and Paris. The questions raised by this literally hard evidence of changing nature led to the first inklings of organic evolution. Studies of the bones by such eminent anatomists as Georges Cuvier of Paris revealed that giant beasts, including wooly mammoths, mastodons, 10-foot-tall sloths, and moose had perished here. What had happened to them?

The scientifically inclined President Thomas Jefferson reasoned they had migrated to the uncharted West as humans populated the Ohio Valley. One of his motivations for launching the Lewis and Clark expedition was to find the still-living representatives of the species whose bones had been unearthed in Kentucky. Many of these were prized possessions in Jefferson's Monticello specimen cabinets.

When the Corps of Discovery returned without any reports of mammoth sightings, the implications were clear. The kinds of animals that roamed the earth had changed over time. The intellectual seeds for the concept of evolution had been germinated at Big Bone Lick. Half a century later, in 1859, English naturalist Charles Darwin explained how evolution happened in *The Origin of Species* and launched the science of biology by codifying its organizing principle.

The fame of the fossil site was such that the founder of modern geology, Scotsman Charles Lyell, visited Big Bone Lick in 1842. Lyell's *Principles of Geology,* with its mountains of evidence for an ancient and changing planet, had been favorite reading of the young Darwin on his famous voyage aboard the HMS *Beagle.* From Lyell, Darwin knew that evolution, by the generations-long process of natu-

ral selection, had time to work.

The mammoths, mastodons, giant sloths, and company lived here during the last ice age. When you visit today's park, you will get a glimpse of its Pleistocene eco- system. A life-size diorama featur- ing these animals is located near the park's museum. Walk along an elevated boardwalk and back 10,000 to 15,000 years to the re- created bog.

Big Bone Lick enjoyed a central place in human culture, too. Both American Indians and white pio- neers set up salt-extraction opera- tions here. In the first half of the 19th century, the sulfur springs gave rise to spa development, and people seeking the suppos- edly curative powers of the stinky mineral water supported a thriv- ing hotel. Only one small, greasy- looking gray spring remains today, and it is unlikely you will be tempted to drink from it.

Be sure to include a visit to the park's current big residents

The bog diorama at Big Bone Lick State Park contains life-size replicas of mastodons and other prehistoric mammals.

A bison rolling in the grass is a member of the park's herd.

in your itinerary. A bison herd roams one corner of the property, providing a living link with the salt lick's past. You can view them from a fenced road-side, accessible by a 10-minute walk from the museum and nature center parking lot.

FACILITY DETAILS

Museum: Even though an enormous number of fossils recovered at Big Bone Lick in the 19th and 20th centuries were shipped elsewhere, there are still some left, and they are on display here. Yes, 10-pound mastodon teeth are impressive. You can get a close look at one anatomical difference between a mammoth and a mastodon from these teeth. "Mastodon" means "breast-shaped tooth." Note the cone-shaped ridges on the mastodon molars; hence the name.

Nature Center: Next door to the museum, the center is open from late spring to early fall. There are displays about current plants and animals found in northern Kentucky. The park naturalist conducts a variety of interpretive programs from the center.

Gift Shop: Located at the museum entrance, the shop stocks books about paleontology and natural history as well as a selection of fossils. You can buy a plush bison, too.

Campground: Contains 62 wooded sites with two shower and laundry facilities, a playground, and a swimming pool for campers' use only. Grocery store is open April 1–October 31.

Trails: Three and a half miles of trails wind around the museum area and circle the lake. From the bog diorama, walk north along the trail and follow your nose through the woods to the remaining sulfur spring. That rotten egg smell is unmistakable. There are signs along the way describing the salt making and spa history of Big Bone Lick. You can help your nose recover by following the loop west and south back to the museum through meadows filled with sweet-scented wildflowers.

Fishing: Bank fishing is permitted on the 7.5-acre lake for catfish, bluegill, largemouth bass, and other species stocked by the state. This is a very peaceful lake, reached by a short uphill hike from a parking lot.

Other Recreation: Eighteen-hole miniature golf course, tennis courts, basketball courts, picnic shelters, softball fields, horseshoe pits.

Special Events: Easter Egg Hunt (March or April), Winter Festival in July, Pirate Week (August), Salt Festival (October).

MORE TO EXPLORE

For a detailed history of the fossil discoveries at the site, read *Big Bone Lick: The Cradle of American Paleontology* by Stanley Hedeen (University Press of Kentucky). The park gift shop stocks it. If you are interested in the general geology and paleontology of the region, head across the Ohio River to the Museum of Natural History and Science at the Cincinnati Museum Center. About a half hour's drive from the park, it has excellent exhibits on the geological history of the Ohio Valley. Go to http://www.cincymuseum.org/ for details.

BLUE LICKS BATTLEFIELD STATE RESORT PARK

10299 Maysville Road
Carlisle, KY 40311
(859) 289-5507 or (800) 443-7008
http://www.parks.ky.gov/findparks/resortparks/bl/
580 acres

FIELDS OF TALL yellow goldenrod and deep purple ironweed are one of Kentucky's most beautiful late summer natural features. The showy blooms are so widespread and so familiar that goldenrod is the official state flower.

In reality, as any botanist will tell you, there are many kinds of goldenrod. Kentucky has no fewer than 34 species of the plants belonging to the genus *Solidago*. Some are common and conspicuous. Others are not. A 55-acre state nature preserve set aside within Blue Licks Battlefield State Resort Park is almost the only place in the world where the federally endangered Short's goldenrod, *Solidago shortii*, grows.

Unlike most of its botanical cousins, Short's goldenrod is small and delicate, growing close to the ground. (That is not where it got the name, however. Dr. Charles Short, a 19th-century Kentucky botanist and physician, first described it.) You will see the plant, with a slender arc of tiny yellow blossoms, growing along the 0.2-mile Buffalo Trace Trail in late August and September. Originally beaten by the mastodons that came to the area's salt lick, this trampled pathway was later used by bison for the same purpose.

Along an old bison trace in the Kentucky state nature preserve within Blue Licks Battlefield State Resort Park is one of the few places in the world where the federally endangered Short's goldenrod grows.

An annual reenactment pays tribute to the pioneers who fought and died at the Battle of Blue Licks, August 19, 1782. The soldiers in green coats were American colonists fighting on the side of the British in the Revolutionary War.

The little flower may grow here because of an ecological association with the large animals and the habitat they created. Botanists admit that they are not sure.

The endangered plant and the prehistoric salt source are not the only rare features of the park. The park's name commemorates one of the few remaining combat sites from the Revolutionary War. It was a battle that involved Kentucky's most famous pioneer, Daniel Boone. And technically, it happened after the war was over. Cornwallis had surrendered to Washington at Yorktown months before, on October 19, 1781. But news from the other side of the Appalachians was slow in getting to frontier Kentucky, and neither the British troops and their American Indian allies nor the colonists were aware that they were living in a new country.

In August 1782, British soldiers and Shawnees attacked Bryan's Station, a settlement near Lexington. As they retreated from the scene, a trio of Kentucky militia commanders, Boone among them, decided to give chase. On August 19, the Kentuckians were ambushed in the woods near the Licking River. Among the 70 militiamen killed was Israel Boone, Daniel's 23-year-old son. Overwhelmed, the Kentuckians were forced to retreat across the river. The disastrous engagement lasted only a few minutes.

Each August on or near the date, the battle is re-created at the park. The neighing of charging horses, the smell and smoke from the exploding gunpowder of long rifles, and heart-stopping war whoops of American Indians fill the air. As the dead fall to the ground, Shawnees take scalps, and the colonial militia commanders shout orders in the chaos.

One feature of the battle you might find puzzling is that the British troops wear green coats, not red. Go to the park museum, where you will learn that Americans who were loyal to the crown fought for the British in green uniforms.

FACILITY DETAILS

Lodge: The contemporary Worthington Lodge has 32 rooms with balconies looking out into the woods. You may very well spot racoons, skunks, foxes, deer, and other wildlife moving around behind the building. The Hidden Waters Restaurant features a seafood buffet the first Friday of every month.

Cottages: Two modern, fully ADA-compliant cottages are located at the north end of the park. Each has two bedrooms.

Campground: The 51 sites are found at the center of the park. All have utilities hookups. Open from mid-March to mid-November.

Right and facing page: The Tanner Station pioneer encampment.

Museum: The Pioneer Museum has a wide variety of displays, including exhibits featuring mastodon bones and American Indian and Kentucky pioneer artifacts. A large portion of the museum is devoted to the Battle of Blue Licks, with uniforms, weapons, and a diorama showing the battlefield terrain. The museum shop stocks a good selection of books on both the pioneer and natural history of the region.

Trails: In addition to the 0.2-mile Buffalo Trace Trail, other park trails include the Savannah Loop (0.5 mile) and the Indian Loop Trail (0.8 mile). The Heritage Trail (2.5 miles) passes by a small, re-created trader's fort, Tanner Station. The Licking River Trail is a 1-mile loop trail to the Licking River that passes near the place where Daniel Boone and his men were captured by Shawnees on a salt-making expedition in 1778.

Boating: Weekly canoe trips are offered in the summer along the Licking River, which bounds the park on three sides. Check with the staff about overnight canoe camping trips, too.

Other Recreation: The park has an 18-hole miniature golf course, a junior Olympic-size pool, a baseball field, an archery range, and two picnic shelters (one with restrooms). Tables, grills, and playgrounds are located throughout the park.

Special Events: Herb and Garden Days (March), Highway 68/80 400-Mile Sale (June), Battle of Blue Licks Reenactment (August), Short's Goldenrod Festival (September).

MORE TO EXPLORE

Another unique northern Kentucky attraction is the tiny river town of Augusta, about an hour's drive from the park. Two dozen 18th- and 19th-century buildings face the Ohio River where a ferry still takes passengers and their cars to the opposite shore and back. In addition to charming shops and restaurants in Augusta, you can visit the Rosemary Clooney House. The singer and actress, a native of nearby Maysville, bought the 1850 house as a second home. (The first was in Beverly Hills.) It is now a museum devoted to her life and career, founded by former Miss America and Augusta native Heather French Henry. If you are too young to remember Rosemary, you will probably know her nephew. Actor George Clooney grew up in Augusta and graduated from the local high school. For visitor information, go to http://www.augustaky.com/.

BOONE STATION
STATE HISTORIC SITE

240 Gentry Road
Lexington, KY 40502
(859) 263-1073
http://www.parks.ky.gov/findparks/histparks/bs/
46 acres

B Y THE LATE 1770S, Fort Boonesborough, near Richmond, had become a
thriving community. This meant it was too crowded for founder Daniel
Boone, who could spend weeks at a time in the wilderness without missing
human companionship. So in 1779, Boone moved his family to land in Fay-
ette County, near Lexington, and with a handful of other families established Boone Station.

A sulphur butterfly feeds on an aster during late summer in Boone Station State Historic
Site's bluegrass savannah.

Boone, his wife Rebecca, and five of their children who still lived at home occupied a double log cabin. Among the other families at Boone Station were those of the Boones' married daughters, Jemima and Rebecca. Unfortunately, by 1781, Boone's claim to the land turned out to be invalid, and by 1791, Boone Station was gone. Boone eventually moved to Missouri, where he died in 1820.

The only trace of the pioneer settlement on the property today is a small cenotaph honoring five members of the Boone family. Otherwise the park is simply a lovely slice of manicured bluegrass pasture, enclosed by the board fences typical of horse farm country. In fact, all that is needed to complete the picture is a few grazing Thoroughbreds. The only facilities, as such, are a scattering of picnic tables. So Boone Station is a fine, peaceful place to stop for a picnic lunch if you are touring the Bluegrass region.

After lunch, stretch your legs along a one-mile trail that winds through the park. In summer, you will see butterflies such as fritillaries, clouded and orange sulphurs, and cabbage whites feeding in the stands of goldenrod and tall asters along the trail.

Special Event: Frontier Stations under Attack (April).

MORE TO EXPLORE

Daniel Boone's colorful life inspired many stories and tall tales. If you are interested in sorting fact from fiction, there are a couple of very good biographies from which to choose: John Mack Faragher's *Daniel Boone: The Life and Legend of an American Pioneer* (Henry Holt and Company) and Robert Morgan's *Boone: A Biography* (Algonquin Books/A Shannon Ravenel Book).

CONSTITUTION SQUARE
STATE HISTORIC SITE

134 South Second Street
Danville, KY 40422
(859) 239-7089
http://www.parks.ky.gov/findparks/histparks/cs/
3 acres

D ANVILLE, ITS TREE-SHADED STREETS lined with stately antebellum and Victorian homes, is one of Kentucky's most charming towns. It is known today as the location of prestigious Centre College and the annual Great American Brass Band Festival. More than 200 years ago, in the 1780s and early 1790s, it was the birthplace of Kentucky's statehood.

The center of that political activity was this square block now surrounded by a bustling downtown. If you visit Constitution Square on a weekday between September and May, you will probably be sharing the space with busloads of schoolchildren. The historic site is a prime field trip destination where students can get a big dose of Kentucky history in a small space.

The meetinghouse at Constitution Square State Historic Site.

Log, brick, and frame buildings are spaced around the square, sheltered by old oaks and hickories. They include a courthouse, a log jail, a meeting-house (which housed the first Presbyterian congregation in Kentucky), a schoolhouse, a post office (the first west of the Appalachians), and Grayson's Tavern. It was in the last building, as you might well imagine, that 30 or so members of Danville's Political Club held most of the meetings that eventually led to a series of state constitutional conventions.

In 1784, Colonel Benjamin Logan organized the first meeting of citizens to discuss the process of making Kentucky a state separate from Virginia. Many had already arrived in Danville for proceedings at the district courthouse. But that first step toward statehood was interrupted by a rumor of an impending attack by American Indians, and the meeting disbanded.

Over the next eight years, nine more constitutional conventions were held, finally resulting in Kentucky becoming the 15th state on June 1, 1792. The delegates to the convention elected Isaac Shelby as the state's first governor.

Shelby and every other Kentucky governor are honored by the Governor's Circle in the northwest corner of the square. At the center of the monument is a six-foot-tall bronze statue of the frock-coated statesman and the buckskin-clad frontiersman who appear on the state seal and flag. Arranged below the figures are concentric brick circles containing evergreen shrubs separating bronze plaques depicting each governor. They are in chronological order. Shelby and A. B.

The Kentucky state seal is reproduced by the statues at the center of the Governor's Circle.

"Happy" Chandler have two plaques each, for their separate terms in office. There is only one woman among the governors—Martha Layne Collins, whose term in office was 1983–1987.

While park staff give guided tours of Constitution Square to school groups, individual visitors are encouraged to stop in the park's information center in the Alban Goldsmith House to pick up a map and brochure for a self-guided tour. There is no charge.

FACILITY DETAILS

Museum Store: Located in the Alban Goldsmith House on the southwest corner of the square. In addition to craft items, candy, and postcards, you can pick up a brochure with detailed information about the history and buildings of Constitution Square. Goldsmith, a physician, was a student of Ephraim McDowell (see More to Explore).

Recreation: Picnic tables are located throughout the square. There are also a couple of wooden gazebos and centrally placed buildings housing public restrooms.

Special Events: Constitution Square Festival (September).

MORE TO EXPLORE

Across Second Street from the square, you will see a white frame, federal-style house with a sign identifying it as the Dr. Ephraim McDowell House and Apothecary. It was here in 1809 that a young doctor from Virginia, educated at Scotland's University of Edinburgh, made medical history. McDowell (who had married Sarah Shelby, daughter of Kentucky's first governor) performed the first successful removal of an abdominal tumor and established himself as the world expert in abdominal surgical techniques. Tour the restored house, apothecary, and gardens for all the gory details. Information is at http://www.mcdowellhouse.com/.

E. P. "TOM" SAWYER STATE PARK

3000 Freys Hill Road
Louisville, KY 40241
(502) 429-7270
http://www.parks.ky.gov/findparks/recparks/ep/
513 acres

ON A WARM, CLEAR FRIDAY night in September, a field at the edge of this park in suburban Louisville is dotted with hard-to-distinguish large, lumpy shapes. There are no lights, but there is a murmur of excited chatter. "I can see some moons!" "Look at the colors!"

The Louisville Astronomical Society hosts public sky viewings at the Urban Astronomy Center at E. P. "Tom" Sawyer State Park.

This is a meeting of the Louisville Astronomical Society, a gathering of sky enthusiasts who maintain the Urban Astronomy Center at E. P. "Tom" Sawyer State Park and invite the public to join them several times a year. Many make their own telescopes (the lumpy objects in the field), and all are happy to explain to anyone who asks a question every detail about the celestial objects on view.

When I visited, Jupiter and Saturn, the solar system's two largest planets, were visible in the western sky. The park is less than 20 miles from the bright lights of downtown Louisville, but it was pitch black out there, and experienced star and planet gazers, including grade school students and retirees, patiently helped newcomers to find the right points of light.

The Urban Astronomy Center is just one of dozens of activities in this park, which acts as a pub-

The running path is one of many recreational facilities at E. P. "Tom" Sawyer State Park.

lic athletic and social club for the residents of Kentucky's largest city. Swimming, soccer, tennis, lacrosse, volleyball, and softball facilities are beautifully maintained and always busy. The one-mile fitness trail that loops through the grounds is popular with both walkers and joggers. Four-legged exercisers are accommodated, too. A special dog park, divided into separate sections for small and large dogs, is located in the northeast corner of the grounds. Another portion of the park, which was carved out of open farmland, is perfectly suited as a radio-controlled model airplane field. There is an archery range, too, as well as picnic facilities and a recreation center.

One feature unique to the state park system is a championship-level BMX track. This competitive extreme cycling is about as far from the quiet pleasures of astronomy as you can imagine. Padded, helmeted riders race up and down the hilly dirt course, testing and jumping their specially designed bikes to the cheers of spectators and loudspeaker reports from an announcer. Most of the participants are 10 to 20 years old, and the vast majority are male. BMX racing became an Olympic sport in 2008.

Racers start down the course in the Grand National BMX competition.

Every August, Sawyer State Park is the site of the National Bicycle League Grand Nationals, which attracts hundreds of riders from around the world. An impromptu camp springs up on the grounds at the edge of the track. As you make your way through this tangle of RVs and tents to join the spectators in the bleachers, be careful not to get run over by a practicing cyclist.

Some park programs are free, and others have fees. Check with the staff.

FACILITY DETAILS

Swimming: An Olympic-size, outdoor pool is open Memorial Day through Labor Day. Classes are held in the morning with public hours in the afternoon.

Sports Fields and Courts: There are 10 soccer and lacrosse fields, 3 lighted softball fields, and 12 tennis courts. Leagues and lessons for various levels are featured in summer.

Trails: In addition to the 1-mile fitness trail (which has 10 exercise stations), the park has a 1.25-mile, easy-grade nature trail that winds through woods and meadows and along Goose Creek.

BMX Track: The BMX track is considered one of the top in the United States. In addition to the NBL Grand Nationals in August, races are held most weekends from the beginning of March until the end of October. Bikers can practice on the track during the week.

Other Recreation: Exercise programs, model airplane field, arts and crafts classes, dog park, seniors' activities, archery range, picnic tables.

Special Events: Irish Classic 10-K Run, National Kite Month Kick-Off (March), Park Triathlon (August), NBL Grand Nationals (August), arts and crafts workshops (several times a year).

MORE TO EXPLORE

If you want to become a regular stargazer at the park, you can join the Louisville Astronomical Society by downloading a membership form from http://louisville-astro. org. For more information about the sport of BMX, go to the National Bicycle League Web site, http://www.nbl.org/, or the Derby City BMX site, http://www.derbycitybmx.com/.

By the way, the park is named in honor of former Jefferson County judge executive Erbon Powers Sawyer. One of his daughters is television journalist Diane Sawyer, who began her career as the "weather girl" at a Louisville news station.

The National Bicycle League's Grand National BMX competition is held every year at E. P. "Tom" Sawyer State Park's motocross course.

FORT BOONESBOROUGH STATE PARK

4375 Boonesborough Road
Richmond, KY 40475
(859) 527-3131
http://www.parks.ky.gov/findparks/recparks/fb/
153 acres

I
F YOU ARE FASCINATED by the life and legend of frontiersman Daniel
Boone, this should be your first Kentucky Boone stop. Not only is the fort
here, but there is also a museum with exhibits on all aspects of Boone's life
and career.

The replica of Fort Boonesborough, built using more than 10,000 logs, is
imposing, the walls of the stockade rising high into the air. But it gives an
impression of vulnerability, too, one that could well have been shared by
the pioneer families who made their homes within the fort in the 1770s. It
is hemmed in on three sides by the forest, and it is not hard to imagine the
uneasiness its residents might have felt knowing that the walls had been
built to protect them from both enemy British troops and hostile American
Indians.

Numerous movies, television shows, books, paintings, and plays provide
impressions of what life was like in Boonesborough. Thanks to the parks
system, visitors to the fort can be immersed in the pioneer existence.

You can wander among the many cabins and other buildings where
costumed interpreters, reenactors, and craftspeople toil away in an 18th-
century mode from April through October.

Men and women are purposefully engaged in all the activities they
would have needed to sustain themselves in the wilderness. The contents
of iron kettles containing ash and lye are being stirred over fires. The result
will be soap, not soup. Buckskin-clad carpenters and gunsmiths lean over
their benches plying their respective crafts. Fabric is spun, woven on looms,
and stitched into rugs and blankets. The fort smells of wood and charcoal
smoke, and the residents themselves look as if they could use hot baths in
the company of some of that newly made soap.

But the real residents would not have had to make quite everything.
Although there was obviously no such thing as ordering up new outdoor
gear from a favorite catalog, one of the buildings at Boonesborough contained goods from the Transylvania Company, the land and trading company founded by Richard Henderson that employed Daniel Boone to found

The reenactment of the siege of Boonesborough.

a settlement. It has the distinction of being the first store in Kentucky, and it, along with other Boonesborough buildings, has been re-created.

And there was time out for a little relaxation. You will see and hear occasional music in the fort, courtesy of pioneers strumming on lutes and guitars.

The domestic routines of the Boonesborough populace were rudely interrupted on more than one occasion, most severely in the fall of 1778. That was when American Indians laid siege to the fort for nine days and nights. Thanks to the determination of the pioneers—and a large supply of gunpowder and ammunition—the attackers finally gave up and left. You can experience the siege in September, when an annual reenactment takes place at the fort.

Even with its good start, Boonesborough did not last. When the Revolutionary War ended, the fort was no longer necessary. Boone and members of his family moved on. By the 1820s, the town was abandoned.

FACILITY DETAILS

Museum: Located near Lock and Dam 10, the Kentucky River Museum's exhibits recount the stories of workers and their families who staffed the locks and dams along the Kentucky River in the early 1900s and the development of the Kentucky and Ohio rivers as important routes of commerce. Like the fort itself, the museum is open April 1 through October 31.

Gift Shop: An impressive selection of books about Daniel Boone can be found here. Products produced in the fort are also for sale, including quilts, hand-dipped candles, lye soap, and pottery. The shop is open April 1–November 30.

Campground: Before the fort was built, Boone and his compatriots camped by the banks of the Kentucky River, and you can, too. The wooded campground has 167 sites, most with electricity and water hookups, but if you are seeking a more authentic Boone experience, there are some primitive tent camping sites, as well. The service building has showers, restrooms, and laundry facilities. Campground is open year-round.

Swimming: A junior Olympic-size swimming pool has a water slide, misty fountain, children's area, and rain tree. A sand beach is available for sunbathing, but be advised that wading in the river is not safe because of pollu-

Artisans, shopkeepers, and other pioneers in period costumes populate the buildings inside Fort Boonesborough.

tion and currents. The pool and beach are open daily Memorial Day to mid-August and weekends only from mid-August through Labor Day.

Trails: The self-guided Kentucky Riverwalk Trail highlights native plants and prehistoric, historic, and geological sites dotted along it. You can also walk the wooded Pioneer Forge Trail and Fort Trail between the fort and the swimming and camping areas of the park.

Fishing and Boating: The Kentucky River contains bluegill, bass, catfish, and other species. Boat launch ramps are available in the park, or you can fish from the bank.

Other Recreation: An 18-hole miniature golf course is just outside the campground check-in. Three picnic shelters, tables, grills, and a playground are located throughout the park.

Special Events: Fireside Chats by actors depicting historic figures (February), 18th Century Trade Fair (May), Kentucky River Heritage Weekend (June), Women on the Frontier (June), Living History—18th Century Military/Militia Muster (July), Siege of Boonesborough Reenactment (September), Hammer-In blacksmithing workshop (October), Winter Trade Days (November).

MORE TO EXPLORE

Hall's on the River is a local watering hole perched on the bank of the Kentucky River just a few minutes from the park; you will see billboards pointing the way. For a pleasant lunch, have a fried fish sandwich while sitting on one of the covered decks overlooking the water and the opposite cliff face. For information, go to http://www.hallsontheriver.com/.

GENERAL BUTLER
STATE RESORT PARK

1608 U.S. Highway 227
Carrollton, KY 41008
(502) 732-4384 or (866) 462-8853
http://www.parks.ky.gov/findparks/resortparks/gb/
791 acres; 30 lake acres

THE PARK IS NAMED in honor of General William Orlando Butler. A member of a prominent military family (his father served under Washington in the Revolutionary War), Butler distinguished himself during the War of 1812, serving with Andrew Jackson in the Battle of New Orleans and in the Mexican War, of which he was the final commander in chief.

At home in Carrollton, he practiced law, published poetry, and ran for public office several times, serving as a U.S. congressman from 1839 to 1843. Other political ventures were less successful. Butler was defeated in his bids to be governor. And he ran for vice president on the ticket with Lewis Cass of Michigan in 1848, but Zachary Taylor and Millard Fillmore prevailed in that election.

You would think, with such a colorful namesake, this park would be buzzing with activity. Certainly during some of its big weekend festivals, as well as the Fourth of July fireworks show, it is a lively place. But most of the time, Butler State Resort Park provides less stirring stimulation.

The lodge and most of the grounds sit at the top of wooded hills providing vistas of the Ohio Valley and the town of Carrollton below. It feels as if it is above and away from the surrounding countryside. In fact, the slopes are so steep that, for a few years in the last century, the park system operated a ski facility here. The combination of climate, the expense of artificial snow, and Kentuckians' general unfamiliarity with the sport ultimately proved the venture impractical.

Facing page: Fourth of July fireworks at General Butler State Resort Park.

Today, visitors can hike the wooded trails along the ridges and cliff edges or indulge in a round of golf on the cozy nine-hole course. Spring is a wonderful time to visit, when purple blossoms of redbuds and pink and white flowering dogwoods provide color against the gray and green hillsides. The small lake is perfect for gliding around in a paddleboat, which can be rented at the park dock.

A train ride is a good way to see the landscape.

A miniature train, whose bell its engineer delights in ringing, chugs along a track next to the lake in season. Be prepared for your little ones to beg to go on a ride. The good news is that you will enjoy it, too.

The lake, as well as the stone overlook in the park, was one of many projects in the park system built in the 1930s by the Civilian Conservation Corps. That this is one of Kentucky's oldest state parks may come as a surprise, because it has one of the most modern lodges.

FACILITY DETAILS

Lodge: The stone, wood, and glass Butler Lodge is built on a hilltop overlooking a sea of green. Looking out the tall windows from the spacious lobby or high-ceilinged restaurant, you feel as if you are in a giant, modern tree house. Each of the 53 rooms has a private balcony or patio overlooking the park swimming pool or a wooded hillside.

Cottages: Two dozen cottages include some with private balconies or patios. One-, two-, and three-bedroom cottages with one bathroom and two- and three-bedroom executive cottages with two bathrooms are available. All are located in a wooded setting near the lake.

Campground: The campground has 111 campsites with utilities hookups and grills. Two service buildings have showers and restrooms, and there is one laundry facility. Open year-round, but some sites are available only from mid-March to mid-November.

Museum: The red brick, Greek revival Butler-Turpin Historic Home was built in 1859 by members of Carroll County's Butler family. Generations of Butlers served the United States as officers in the Revolutionary War, the War of 1812, the Mexican War, and the Civil War. Their histories are featured on tours of the house, which is furnished with period antiques and personal effects of the family. Situated on a low hill and bounded by a dry-stacked stonewall, the grounds of the house also contain a family cemetery. The grave of the park's namesake, General William Orlando Butler, is there.

Conference Center: Located north of the lodge, the center has 7,500 square feet of meeting space distributed over three rooms: the Bluegrass Room (with a wall of windows opening onto a terrace), Commonwealth Room, and Kentucky Room (with a working fireplace).

The tall windows in the atrium of the hilltop lodge at General Butler State Resort Park give visitors the feeling of being in a giant tree house.

Trails: The park has about 6 miles of hiking trails. They vary from 0.25 to 4.5 miles in length and all connect, so you can design as long or as short a walk as you wish. Bear in mind that there are some steep grades. The Woodland Trail is especially good for spring wildflowers, and you may see such species along it as mayapple and Dutchman's breeches, as well as several kinds of ferns. The Fossil Trail has easily spotted marine fossils embedded in limestone along the route, which winds past the ruins of the former ski lodge and to the stone overlook built by the CCC in the 1930s. From this vantage point, you can look down on the town of Carrollton and see where the Kentucky River flows into the Ohio River. If you do not fancy a hike, you can drive up a paved road to the overlook instead.

Fishing and Boating: Fishing for bluegill, bass, crappie, and catfish is permitted from the shore of the lake and from nonmotorized boats. You can also enjoy the water in a pedal boat, canoe, or rowboat rented from the boat dock.

Golf Course: Designers managed to squeeze a nine-hole golf course with pro shop onto the one relatively flat patch of land in the park.

Other Recreation: Picnic area, playground, tennis, basketball courts, and shelter house are located near the Butler-Turpin Historic Home, and the campground has a playground and basketball and volleyball courts.

Special Events: Spirits of Butler Paranormal Weekend (April, September), Kentucky Scottish Weekend (May), Summer Saturday Outdoor Movies (June, July), Fireworks over Butler Lake (weekend closest to Fourth of July), American Roots Concert Series (July–October), Kentucky Flyer Railroad Train Show (August), Goldenrod Gala (August), Tales of the Butler Ghosts (October), Festival of Trees and Winter Wonderfest Day (December).

MORE TO EXPLORE

When you have finally had your fill of bucolic peace and quiet at this hilly retreat, you can head up I-71 for NASCAR and other auto racing at the Kentucky Speedway near Sparta. For details, go to http://www. kentuckyspeedway.com/. The track is less than 20 miles from the park. You can get there in about 15 minutes if you put the pedal to the metal, but when a state trooper pulls you over, you did not hear this from me.

Knob Lick Pike, 5.5 miles south of Danville on U.S. 127
near Junction City, KY 40440
(859) 239-7089 (Constitution Square)
http://www.parks.ky.gov/findparks/histparks/cs/ (Constitution Square)
0.25 acre

ISAAC SHELBY, military hero in the Revolutionary War and the War of 1812, frontier statesman, and Kentucky's first and fifth governor, was so widely respected in his lifetime that counties and towns in no fewer than three states are named in his honor. So it is quite a paradox that the smallest property in the state park system, a tiny quarter of an acre, is devoted to Shelby's life and career.

The site, once part of Shelby's estate, which he named Traveller's Rest, is reached by a private, tree-lined farm road off Knob Lick Pike. (There are signs from U.S. 127.) It consists of the family cemetery, several panels detailing the governor's life and career, a couple of picnic tables, and a six-car parking lot. Corn grows in the fields on the other side of the wood-plank fences surrounding the state property. The main house, built after the original dwelling burned in 1905, is visible in the distance.

The little park still makes a pleasant traveler's rest today. Relax at one of the picnic tables and listen to the rustle of the corn, the calls of bobwhites, and the chattering of starlings. One or two of the farm's dogs may saunter up the lane to give you a tail-wagging greeting with the expectation of a friendly ear rub in return.

Take your time to read about Shelby's notable contributions to national and state history. Among many other achievements, he was instrumental in the drafting of Kentucky's state constitution and was so respected by his constitutional colleagues that they unanimously chose him to be the first governor. During his second term, which coincided with the War of 1812, he personally raised 3,200 troops from the state and led them to join General William Henry Harrison's army to defeat the British at the Battle of the Thames in Ontario. It was the decisive victory of the war. Shelby was 62 years old at the time.

It is possible to look over the chest-high stone wall into the cemetery, but visitors are not permitted to enter. The gate is locked. The most conspicuous marker, a white stone monument in the far corner, is the gravesite of Shelby

Isaac Shelby Cemetery State Historic Site is located on the former estate of Kentucky's first governor.

and his wife Susannah. Isaac Shelby was a native of Maryland, and Susannah Hart was born in North Carolina. Appropriately, the future first First Couple of Kentucky met at Fort Boonesborough.

MORE TO EXPLORE

The Isaac Shelby site is one of four state parks and historic sites within a few miles of one another along U.S. 127. None has overnight accommodations. But if you want to stay in the area to explore the attractions, book a room at the historic Beaumont Inn in Harrodsburg. Rooms in the antebellum mansion are furnished with antiques, and the dining room specializes in fine southern cooking, including real fried chicken, country ham, and corn pudding. Details can be found at http://www.beaumontinn.com/.

KINCAID LAKE STATE PARK

565 Kincaid Park Road
Falmouth, KY 41040
(859) 654-3531
http://www.parks.ky.gov/findparks/recparks/kl/
919 acres; 183 lake acres

WHEN YOU TURN into the entrance of Kincaid Lake State Park, the road takes you right through the center of the park's newest facility, a nine-hole golf course that opened in 2004. The fairways are visible on either side of the road. Just beyond the modern golf course, you will come to the park office, one of the oldest buildings in use in the park system. The little log cabin was built in 1878, and if you look closely, you will see that it is held together by dovetailed joints and wooden pegs. No nails.

There are other ways in which Kincaid Lake State Park is a study in contrasts. The swimming pool, built so that it perches over the lake, is awash in sunlight. This is a busy community pool, and the park amphitheater, where movies are shown on weekends in the summer, also attracts a crowd.

The trails in the park, however, offer wooded seclusion and, if you are so inclined, an entomological treasure hunt. The trailhead is near the campground entrance. Walk along the path and you will soon come to a fork. Signs point to the Ironwood Trail and Spicebush Trail, the latter of which begins when you bear right across a wooden bridge.

This is your hunting ground. You are searching for the spicebush swallowtail (*Papilio troilus*), a beautiful black and iridescent blue butterfly common in this patch of woods because the food plant for its caterpillar, the common spicebush (*Lindera benzoin*), grows here in abundance.

The swimming pool at Kincaid Lake State Park overlooks the lake.

You will smell the aromatic bushes yourself, especially on a warm day. In the middle of the summer, the butterflies, with their distinctive twin streamer tails, glide among the trees in purposeful flight paths. But when you come to spicebush plants, take time for a careful search for the caterpillars.

Like most butterfly and moth larvae, the spicebush swallowtail caterpillars go through several molts, called instars, and so change color and form as they mature. The younger stages resemble gray and white bird droppings, which obviously affords them excellent protective camouflage from hungry predators.

The real prize will be to spot one of the last instar caterpillars. Their survival strategy is far more aggressive. About the size of your thumb, the bright green caterpillar, edged with yellow, has large black, yellow, and white eyespots. You may see one waving its head in a wonderful imitation of a tiny snake.

Kincaid Lake has much more conspicuous wildlife, too. If you choose to sunbathe by the pool, check the nearby meadow for white-tailed deer. The waterside grasses provide a favorite grazing site. And do not be surprised if you look up from your grill to see a wild turkey wandering through the campground.

A wild turkey takes a stroll through the camping area at Kincaid Lake State Park.

FACILITY DETAILS

Campground: There are 84 sites, including several primitive ones for tents. The best of these are located next to the lake. The sites with utilities hookups have varying amounts of shade. The campground has a grocery, a playground, and a service building with restrooms and showers. Open from mid-March to mid-November.

Trails: The wooded hiking trails form intersecting loops, so you can walk either the 1-mile Spicebush Trail or the 1.5-mile Ironwood Trail or combine them for a longer hike.

A white-tailed doe inspects the camping area from near the shoreline of Kincaid Lake.

Fishing and Boating: The lake has abundant trophy-size largemouth bass, as well as bluegill, channel catfish, crappie, and sunfish. The marina has a launching ramp and 38 open boat slips and rents fishing boats, pontoon boats, rowboats, and pedal boats from April 1 to September 30.

Golf Course: The nine-hole course is laid out on hilly ground with views of the lake from some fairways. The pro shop stocks golfing apparel and rents carts and other equipment.

Buildings: A multipurpose building with seating for 240 can be rented for meetings or other functions. Weekly movies are shown in the summer in the 300-seat amphitheater.

Other Recreation: The lakeside swimming pool with bathhouse is open daily from Memorial Day to mid-August and weekends only from mid-August through Labor Day. The park also has a seasonal nine-hole minia-

A great blue heron near the shore.

ture golf course near the camping area and basketball, volleyball, tennis, handball, and shuffleboard courts. A picnic shelter with restrooms, tables, grills, and a playground overlooks the lake.

MORE TO EXPLORE

A couple of invaluable books to take along when butterfly hunting in the state parks are *Butterflies through Binoculars: The East* by Jeffery Glassberg (Oxford University Press) and *Caterpillars of Eastern North America* by David L. Wagner (Princeton Field Guides). These are available at most commercial bookstores. For specific information about hatching times and locations of Kentucky's insects, use Charles van Orden Covell Jr.'s *The Butterflies and Moths (Lepidoptera) of Kentucky* (Kentucky State Nature Preserves Commission). It can be ordered from the publisher at http://www.naturepreserves.ky.gov/inforesources/Bookstore.htm.

LINCOLN HOMESTEAD STATE PARK

5079 Lincoln Park Road
Springfield, KY 40069
(859) 336-7461
http://www.parks.ky.gov/findparks/recparks/lh/
230 acres; 41 lake acres

I T SEEMS A BIT STRANGE that most of the park dedicated to the courtship of Abraham Lincoln's parents is taken up by a golf course. Honest Abe was not among the many American presidents who have been duffers. But it is an attractive course, and a visit to the buildings on the site, which are bounded by split-rail fences very like the kind that young Abe was famous

for building, will give you a good dose of Lincoln family history. The buildings are open for tours from the beginning of May to the end of September.

The two-story Francis Berry House was moved from its original site about a mile away. It was here that Nancy Hanks was living when Thomas Lincoln courted her. He proposed to her in front of the living room fireplace. The parents of the future president were married in 1806.

The house is furnished with pieces from the period. Pioneer life was not easy, but the home was fairly cozy, if the colorful quilts and rugs accenting the hand-carved furniture and hardwood floors are any

The two-story log Francis Berry House contains pioneer furniture and artifacts from the early 19th century.

Facing page: Teeing off at hole 3 in front of the Francis Berry House at Lincoln Homestead State Park.

indication. The windows have glass, rather than just shutters, which would have added to the inhabitants' comfort. Note the waviness characteristic of the glass made at the time.

A more modest dwelling on the property is a replica of the log cabin where Thomas Lincoln was born, one of five children of Captain Abraham and Bersheba Lincoln. Thomas lived with his parents until he was 25, learning blacksmithing and carpentry skills. A replica blacksmith shop, with antique tools, is among the buildings in the park.

Thomas Lincoln's eldest brother, Mordecai, built a house on the family property that is still here. It stands by itself on its original site, at the far end of the golf course from the other historical structures.

FACILITY DETAILS

Gift Shop: Located in the cluster of 19th-century cabins, the shop stocks Kentucky handicrafts and souvenirs. Like the other buildings, it is open May 1 to September 30.

Golf Course: The 18-hole regulation course is laid out over rolling countryside and along three lakes. You will have the unique experience of teeing off next to log cabins, too. The pro shop rents out carts and other equipment.

Other Recreation: A picnic shelter, tables, grills, restrooms, playground, and parking area are located near the cabins.

MORE TO EXPLORE

An hour's drive from the state site is the National Park Service–maintained Abraham Lincoln Birthplace National Historic Site in Hodgenville. This was the location of Thomas Lincoln's Sinking Spring Farm, and 116 acres of it are preserved here. A small one-room log cabin, thought to be similar to the one in which the 16th president was born on February 12, 1809, is preserved inside a stone memorial building. A museum dedicated to Lincoln's early life in Kentucky features a short film about his life and career. For details, go to http://www.nps.gov/abli/.

MY OLD KENTUCKY HOME STATE PARK

501 East Stephen Foster Avenue
Bardstown, KY 40004
(502) 348-3502
http://www.parks.ky.gov/findparks/recparks/mo/
290 acres

EVERY YEAR on the first Saturday in May, tens of thousands of spectators who have gathered at Churchill Downs in Louisville to watch America's oldest annual sporting event break into song. The sentimental strains of "My Old Kentucky Home" ring out to escort the horses onto the track for the running of the Kentucky Derby.

A large proportion of the day's singers of the official state song are not Kentuckians. That is perfectly fine, since its composer was not one either. Like the racing fans attending the Derby, Pennsylvanian Stephen Collins Foster was a visitor to Kentucky. Like many in the Churchill Downs crowd, he had relatives here. They were his cousins, the Rowan family of Federal Hill in Bardstown.

Judge John Rowan built the handsome red brick Georgian mansion in 1795, a year after his marriage. Its original 13 rooms supposedly represent the original 13 colonies. As well as serving on the district court of appeals, Rowan enjoyed a career as a U.S. senator from Kentucky. No doubt Federal Hill would be a historic landmark today for its architectural interest and Rowan's stature alone. But "My Old Kentucky Home," published in 1852, immortalized the house, which was said to have inspired the song. Legend has it that, a decade later, when soldiers fighting in the Civil War who knew the song saw the house, they referred to Federal Hill as My Old Kentucky Home, and the name stuck.

Stephen Foster has been called the American Mozart. Obviously the music of the two is very different. But Foster was also a tremendously prolific composer—he wrote some 200 songs in the space of 20 years—and he, like Mozart, died tragically young, while still in his 30s.

There is some dispute about whether Foster ever visited Federal Hill, though the Rowans were his relatives and it was very possible he stopped here on his documented trip to New Orleans in 1852. The one confirmed visit of Foster to Kentucky was in 1833, when his mother took seven-year-old

The driver of a horse-drawn carriage chats with guides at My Old Kentucky Home State Park.

Stephen on a visit to family in Augusta and Louisville, both cities located downstream on the Ohio River from Foster's Pittsburgh home.

When you visit My Old Kentucky Home, costumed guides in hoop skirts fill in details about the lives of both Foster and the Rowan family. They have a memorized script, which ensures that every tour is uniformly informative. The house underwent a complete remodeling in 2006 to restore rugs, curtains, and wallpaper to the antebellum period of the house.

As beautiful as the main house is, the most appealing building on the property is Judge Rowan's office. The little log cabin located down the hill from the front of the house is the modest and cozy retreat where he studied classical literature and tutored area law students.

FACILITY DETAILS

Visitor Center and Gift Shop: You enter the park through this neo-Georgian building where admission tickets are sold. It contains a large gift shop and a special events facility. Meeting rooms open onto a large patio

overlooking the gardens and grounds. The house is popular for parties and weddings. The gift shop stocks a large selection of books by Kentucky authors, Kentucky food and craft items, and, of course, recordings of music by Stephen Foster.

Amphitheater: *Stephen Foster: The Musical* is the perennial anchor of the summer theater season (early June to mid-August). The story of the composer's life is framed with 50 of his songs, including "Beautiful Dreamer," "Camptown Races," and, of course, "My Old Kentucky Home." Two or three other productions rotate with the Foster musical. Concerts are held in the amphitheater, too. Call (800) 626-1563 or go to http://www.stephenfoster.com/ for details about this year's season.

Campground: The next road east of the main park entrance leads to the 39-site campground, tucked in the woods with the golf course beyond the trees. The park's playground and picnic facilities are here, too. All sites have utilities hookups, and the service building has showers and restrooms. Open from mid-March to mid-November.

Golf Course: The 18-hole Kenny Rapier Golf Course is named after a Bardstown native, a former state legislator and state parks commissioner. The rolling course is bordered by tall trees, but holes 12, 13, and 14 are within sight of Federal Hill and its gardens. Entrance and pro shop are along the same road as the campground.

Special Events: Christmas Candlelight Tours (November–December).

MORE TO EXPLORE

Besides Stephen Foster, Bardstown's big claim to fame is its self-proclaimed status as Bourbon Capital of the World. The name is justified. There is more bourbon whiskey aging in warehouses in Nelson County than in any other location. Heaven Hill is just outside town, and the distillery has a state-of-the-art visitor center and a barrel-shaped tasting room. The Oscar Getz Museum of American Whiskey is in Bardstown. Both the Jim Beam and Maker's Mark distilleries are located about 30–45 minutes from Bardstown's courthouse square. The Kentucky Bourbon Festival is held in Bardstown every September. For information about these and other bourbon-related attractions in Kentucky, go to http://www.kentuckybourbontrail.com/.

2998 Briar Creek Road
Bee Spring, KY 42259
(270) 286-4240
http://www.parks.ky.gov/findparks/recparks/nl/
333 acres; 5,795 lake acres

L ONGLEAF PINE (*Pinus palustris*) is a beautiful tall, straight tree with almost foot-long needles that grow in bundles from the tips of the tree's twigs. This gives the branches a fluffy, tufted look. These eye-catching trees are valued for timber in their native Deep South and are also an important source of turpentine. Very unusually, they are also found sheltering the tent camping ground at Nolin Lake State Park. As the needles are shed, they leave a soft layer on the campsite floor. You almost want to lie down on them for an afternoon nap.

An after-dinner card game in the campground.

The campground
at Nolin Lake
State Park.

Among the system's newer parks, Nolin Lake State Park opened in 1996, and it still seems fresh and undiscovered, especially on weekdays. The lake by the park is long and narrow and is bounded by a sandy beach reached from the same parking lot that serves the tent camping area.

Just up the hill from the beach, on a low ridge overlooking the lake, is another stand of tall trees, mostly pig hickories and Virginia pine. Several picnic tables are lined up beneath them, providing a perfect place to enjoy a quiet lunch accompanied by the drumming of woodpeckers, the lap of water on the shore, and, sometimes, a jet ski or two.

A fine way to stretch your legs after eating is to take the Waterfall Trail that begins at the end of the picnic area and soak in the sounds of the forest and the lake.

FACILITY DETAILS

Campground: Utilities hookups are available at 32 sites. There are 20 primitive sites for tents. Three sites are ADA compliant. A playground and a shower and restroom building are located in the campground. Open Memorial Day through Labor Day.

Trail: The 1.6-mile Waterfall Trail makes a loop through the woods, along the lake, and past a little waterfall.

Fishing and Boating: Bass, catfish, crappie, and walleye are in the lake. A boat launch ramp is near the campground, but there is no marina.

Other Recreation: A seasonal grocery and restroom building are near a picnic shelter and the campground. Picnic tables have excellent views of the lake.

Special Event: Nolin Fest (August).

MORE TO EXPLORE

Nolin Lake is about a half hour north of Mammoth Cave National Park. The world's longest mapped cave system, 365 miles and counting, is a UNESCO World Heritage Site. Many kinds of cave tours are offered, including special kids-only excursions involving plenty of crawling through mud. For tidier-minded grown-ups, the Frozen Niagara Tour is a fully upright, easygoing introduction to the park's remarkable geology. For details about visiting the park and exploring the cave, go to http://www.nps.gov/maca/.

OLD FORT HARROD STATE PARK

100 South College Street
Harrodsburg, KY 40330-0156
(859) 734-3314
http://www.parks.ky.gov/findparks/recparks/fh/
32 acres

ORT BOONESBOROUGH ENJOYS the frontier name recognition, but the
oldest permanent white settlement in Kentucky, established by pioneer
James Harrod in 1774, was Fort Harrod. That makes the town that grew up
around it, Harrodsburg, the state's first and oldest.

Harrod does not enjoy the same fame as Daniel Boone, perhaps because
of his tragic life and mysterious death. Like Boone, he was born in Pennsylvania, but the exact date is unknown. Many of his family members, including his brother and his father's first wife, were killed in American Indian
raids. During his exploration of the Northwest Territory, he learned several
American Indian languages, plus French, and gained leadership qualities
that made him the choice of other frontierspeople to lead the settlement
that was first known as Harrodstown.

Harrod acquired much of the land in the area and became fairly wealthy.
But by the 1790s, he disappeared on increasingly longer hunting trips. His
stepson was abducted by American Indians and burned at the stake, and
this seemed to further unbalance Harrod. In 1792 he left on another hunting trip and was never seen again.

The historic significance of Harrodsburg spurred the reconstruction of
the fort, nearly on its original footprint, in the 1920s. It has been a popular
destination for school groups and tourists ever since.

The entrance to the stockade is at the top of a broad stone staircase. As
you walk up the steps, you will notice a walled cemetery on your right and
a bas-relief monument on your left. The cemetery is the resting place of 500
people who lived in and near the fort. It is the oldest cemetery west of the
Appalachians. President Franklin D. Roosevelt dedicated the memorial to
the exploration of the Northwest Territory by George Rogers Clark in 1934.

Large blockhouses at its corners anchor the fort. Smaller cabins, which
would have been individual homes, line the walls. These are furnished with
hand-carved tables, chairs, and beds and occupied by guides in period costume, who will tell you about each building and its people. The ground
inside the fort provided the settlement's support services, including a log
schoolhouse. Gardens are planted in beans, squash, and corn, as well as

herbs and flowers. A roofed pen shelters live goats. Indeed, as you enter the fort, you may be as impressed by the strong scents of goats and the coal-fired blacksmith forge as you are by the sights of the settlement.

As you walk along the north side of the fort and down the slope to the northwest corner, you will come across the reason Harrod built the fort here. There is a spring bubbling out of the hillside, an all-important source of water in the event that hostile American Indians trapped the settlers inside the stockade, which indeed happened on several occasions.

That is also why the windows of the cabins face into the fort, making the interiors pretty dark. There are slits high in the walls of the blockhouses through which the barrels of long rifles would have been aimed.

You may want to bring a picnic lunch to have at one of the tables beneath the park's remarkable tree. This is the giant Osage orange that started to

Civil War reenactors at Old Fort Harrod State Park.

A portrait of Mrs.
J. Breckenridge
Viley (circa 1890) by
Harrodsburg artist
May P. Hardin hangs in
the Mansion Museum.

grow here in the late 18th century and so would have been witness to the original fort. Its trunk is split, and its massive branches spread along the ground like the tentacles of a giant, woody octopus. Children—and some adults, including me—cannot resist the urge to climb on it.

In summer, you may want to stay for an evening performance of a play or concert in the James Harrod Amphitheater. It is located just behind the stockade's southwest corner.

FACILITY DETAILS

Museum and Church: Two buildings flank the entrance to the park. The one with the steeple is a church that has inside it the Lincoln Marriage

Temple, the original log cabin where Abraham Lincoln's parents were married on June 12, 1806. The Mansion Museum across from the church contains Civil War artifacts, an antique gun collection, American Indian artifacts, and Lincoln memorabilia.

Amphitheater and Conference Center: These are on the other side of the fort from the parking lot. The center is available for rent. The amphitheater has programs for school groups during the academic year and is a venue for concerts in the summer.

Recreation: Picnic tables are located near the massive Osage orange tree, and there are a shelter and playground behind the fort.

Special Events: Kentucky's Fort Harrod Beef Festival (June), picnics and outdoor concerts (June–August), Fort Harrod Holiday Special (November), Civil War Living History Program (November).

MORE TO EXPLORE

If you wish to linger in the region for a while, consider staying at Shaker Village of Pleasant Hill. It is a short drive from downtown Harrodsburg. Accommodations are available in many buildings of the largest restored Shaker community in the United States. A national historic landmark, it is situated on 3,000 bucolic acres by the Kentucky River. The restaurant, which serves authentic Shaker dishes, is excellent. Save room for the lip-puckering Shaker lemon pie. Details are at http://www.shakervillageky.org/.

PERRYVILLE BATTLEFIELD STATE HISTORIC SITE

1825 Battlefield Road
Perryville, KY 40468
(859) 332-8631
http://www.parks.ky.gov/findparks/histparks/pb/
669 acres

THE MOST IMPORTANT Civil War battle in Kentucky, the Battle of Perryville, took place on October 7–8, 1862. Even though the Bluegrass State had not seceded from the Union, slavery was legal, and regiments from Kentucky fought for both the North and the South. Lincoln was concerned that his native state could be lost at any time. Perryville was significant not only for the political fate of Kentucky, according to Pulitzer Prize–winning historian James McPherson, but also for the course of the war:

> It is scarcely an exaggeration to say that the Confederacy would have won the war if it could have gained Kentucky, and conversely, that the Union's success in retaining Kentucky as a base for invasions of the Confederate heartland brought eventual Union victory.

Soldiers at a ridgetop just before the beginning of the reenactment.

On those two days in October, the Confederate threat to the state was vanquished once and for all. That pivotal piece of geography is preserved at the 669 hilly acres of Perryville Battlefield State Historic Site.

The site is crisscrossed with more than seven miles of trails punctuated by interpretive markers that vividly describe the course of the battle. Standing at the top of Parsons' Ridge on a hot summer afternoon, you will hear only the buzz of insects and the occasional bird call. But as you read the account of the conflict, standing next to a Civil War cannon and gazing down the hill, you will imagine the explosions of gunfire and screams of men and horses.

Union Brigadier General William Terrill was nearly panic-stricken. To his surprise, thousands of Confederates swarmed over the fields in front of you, moving toward the Federal lines. The shouts of attacking Southern troops and the crescendo of gunfire echoed among these hills.

A Union soldier rides in a cavalry charge during the reenactment of the Battle of Perryville.

A costumed reenactor stands near the monument to the Confederate dead at Perryville Battlefield State Historic Site.

The Confederates did not realize that they were vastly outnumbered. They had 16,000 troops, but the Union had 58,000. In the brutal two-day battle, more than 7,500 soldiers were killed or wounded. Confederate general Braxton Bragg finally retreated, taking his soldiers back to Tennessee. Kentucky stayed in the Union.

For an even more vivid experience of the Battle of Perryville, come to the park on the October weekend when uniformed reenactors swarm across the battlefield. Artillery fire echoes over the hills again, and clouds of gun smoke hang in the valleys, illustrating all too well the fog of war.

Troops march toward the battlefield at dawn for the reenactment. Morning fog blends with gunpowder smoke.

FACILITY DETAILS

Museum: Perryville Battlefield Museum has displays of battle artifacts, a map of the battle, and other exhibits about the Civil War. The shop stocks a good selection of books about Perryville in particular and the Civil War in general.

Trails: There are more than 40 interpretive signs at important points along the self-guided trails, which mostly run over open meadow. It is a good idea to take water and wear a hat if the day is sunny and hot. A Confederate monument, erected in 1902, and a Union monument, which followed in 1931, are located near the museum.

A young reenactor at the troops' campgrounds during the reenactment of the Battle of Perryville.

Other Recreation: The park has a picnic shelter with restrooms, tables, grills, and a playground.

Special Events: On the Farm (June), Annual Perryville Battle Reenactment (October).

MORE TO EXPLORE

For a full account of the battle and its historic significance, read *Perryville: This Grand Havoc of Battle* by Kenneth W. Noe (University Press of Kentucky). The park museum shop has it. For information about the annual reenactment, including how to participate if you are a Civil War reenactor, go to the official Battle of Perryville Web site, http://www.perryvillereenactment.org/.

ROUGH RIVER DAM
STATE RESORT PARK

450 Lodge Road
Falls of Rough, KY 40119
(270) 257-2311 or (800) 325-1713
http://www.parks.ky.gov/findparks/resortparks/rr/
637 acres; 4,860 lake acres

Rough River Dam State Resort Park is not among the system's more appealing facilities. The surrounding landscape of Grayson and Breckinridge counties is tired and eroded. The 1960s-era lodge is not aging gracefully, and the trail leading from it around the lake is choked with poison ivy. The park's airfield no longer offers airplane fuel.

But during one weekend in July, you will have more fun at this park than at almost any other. That is when the air is filled with the music of the Official Kentucky State Championship Old Time Fiddlers' Contest. The energy

Musicians jam in the campground during the Official Kentucky State Championship Old Time Fiddlers' Contest at Rough River Dam State Resort Park.

and pure pleasure of the participants, whose age range spans decades, is infectious.

Tractor-drawn shuttles take listeners and musicians from the front of the lodge to a hillside below the dam. At the bottom is a little cabin with a covered front porch, the stage for the music. Listeners bring folding chairs, and bluegrass enthusiasts form pickup bands, circling together with their banjos, mandolins, guitars, fiddles, and harmonicas to trade melodies and improvise harmonies.

On the cabin porch, where a quilt serves as a backdrop, contestants perform one by one in their respective categories. The prize money must be good, because the competition attracts participants from as far away as Florida and Texas. Each musician is announced by a local radio personality who has a seemingly endless stock of corny jokes. A harmonica soloist is accompanied by a guitar and string bass. Fiddlers play unaccompanied or with guitarists. The strains of standards such as "The Tennessee Waltz," "Blues Stay Away from Me," "Too Young to Marry," and "Just a Closer Walk with Thee" echo up the hillside.

The fiddlers' contest is not the only musical event here. In winter, the tunes move indoors during February's Dulcimer Weekend. The park sponsors a slew of other seasonal events that serve the surrounding communities, too.

An original T-34B navy airplane takes off from the airstrip at Rough River Dam State Resort Park.

Anglers in pursuit of quarry during a bass fishing tournament.

Given the emphasis here on traditional music, it is fitting that also found within the park is a Folklore Nature Trail maintained by the U.S. Army Corps of Engineers. Pick up a guidebook from the park lodge and enjoy the wooded, 0.7-mile walk with 27 numbered stations. It starts with a moonshiner's still, appropriate since the park is located in two dry counties, and ends at a log cabin. In between are several species of trees and shrubs that were important to early settlers either as medicinal herbs or as building materials.

FACILITY DETAILS

Lodge: There are 40 rooms, which have patios and balconies facing the lake. The lodge also contains a 167-seat restaurant and several conference rooms.

A catch from a bass fishing tournament at Rough River Dam State Resort Park.

Cottages: There are 17 two-bedroom cottages located in two circles near the lake. The furniture is purely functional, but the water pressure in the showers is notably excellent.

Campground: The 64-site campground is on the wooded edge of Rough River at the north end of the park. All sites have utilities hookups, and the grounds include a central service building.

Airport: This is a 3,200-foot paved, lighted airstrip. Fuel is not available. There is an air camp where you can pitch a tent by your plane. It has a service building with showers and restrooms.

Trails: A 1-mile trail along the lake from the lodge to the marina, a 1-mile circular walk behind the lodge, and a 0.7-mile Folklore Nature Trail are located in the park.

Fishing and Boating: Bank fishing is permitted off the lakeside trail. The marina is open from May through October. It has a launch ramp and rents pontoon boats. The lake is stocked with bluegill, channel catfish, crappie, rough fish, and largemouth, white, and Kentucky bass.

Golf Course: The golf course has nine holes and a driving range. Two of the fairways are lakeside. A pro shop serves the course.

Swimming: The park's swimming pool is next to the lodge. There is also a beach with bathhouse on the lake.

Other Recreation: Archery, canoe trips, volleyball, tennis, shuffleboard, playgrounds, 18-hole miniature golf course, and picnic shelter.

Special Events: Rook Tournament (January), Dulcimer Weekend Festival (February), Square Dance Weekend (February), Buffalo and Wild Game Buffet (March), Youth Bowfishing Tournament (May), Model Airplane Meet (May), Magnolia 5-K Run/Walk (July), Old Time Fiddlers' Contest (July), Rough River Winter Wonderland (November–December).

Water tubing
at Rough River
Dam State
Resort Park.

MORE TO EXPLORE

If you cannot make it to the fiddlers' contest in July, you have not missed
all the music. Every Friday night, about 20 minutes from the park, bluegrass musicians get together to give free concerts in the old Caneyville
school gym or, when the weather is fine, on the Leitchfield courthouse
square. They play for hours. For more information, go to http://www.
graysoncountytourism.com/.

TAYLORSVILLE LAKE STATE PARK

1320 Park Road
Taylorsville, KY 40071
(502) 477-8713
http://www.parks.ky.gov/findparks/recparks/tl/
2,560 acres; 3,050 lake acres

DRIVING ALONG ANY of the major interstates or federal highways in Louisville on a Friday evening or Saturday morning between Memorial Day and Labor Day, you will notice a large number of vehicles towing boats and heading east. Chances are very high that the boaters are heading for Taylorsville Lake, less than an hour from the city, and they probably have fishing gear onboard.

The long, meandering lake opened in 1982 when the Army Corps of Engineers completed the dam it built for flood control of the Salt River. Thanks to strict fishing limits early in the lake's history, the bass, bluegill, catfish, and crappie bred like mad and now thrive in such abundance in the lake that you have to be a very lazy angler indeed not to hook a fish here. Virtually every gas station along the route to the park sells bait, so forgetting your night crawlers is no excuse, either.

Besides being a favorite fishing destination, the park has 16 miles of trails. These are especially popular with horseback riders. If you want to spend the night with your ride, the park has a special horse camping area outfitted with hitching posts and watering troughs. There is immediate access to the trail system just off the horse campground.

Hikers and mountain bikers also use the trails, which circle through the park in an interconnecting network, but there is a distinct advantage to traveling by horse on the park trails lined with young trees and banks of tall wildflowers and grasses. The footfalls of a horse seem not to raise the alert of deer and turkeys the way a two-legged step does. From your horseback vantage point, you may very well see more wildlife on the trails than do walkers and bikers.

FACILITY DETAILS

Facing page:
A sailboat on
Taylorsville Lake.

Campground: The 45-site campground is designed for RVs. There are utilities hookups and a service building. The Horseman's Camp has 10 sites with hookups and horse-related amenities. Open from mid-March to mid-November.

Trails: Individual rails range from 0.5 to 6 miles. All connect for a total of 16 miles. Some are wooded, and many pass through meadows awash in tall asters and goldenrod in summer and fall. The Salt River Vista Loop (2.1 miles) and the Pete Campbell trail (0.6 mile one way) both have scenic overlooks of the lake.

Fishing and Boating: This is the most heavily stocked fishing lake in the state, and a network of coves and inlets provides excellent casting sites. There is an ADA-compliant fishing pier, too. The marina has open and covered slips, fuel, food, and fishing tackle. Fishing boats and pontoon boats are for rent. Taylorsville Lake is also popular with sailboaters. The lake has four launch ramps. Rent a marina fishing boat and schedule cruising time on one of the marina's pontoon boats, or launch your own. Contact the seasonal Taylorsville Lake dock at (502) 477-8766.

Other Recreation: Picnic tables are located throughout the park.

Special Events: Possum Ridge 5-K Run (June).

In addition to several miles of riding trails, Taylorsville Lake State Park has special horse camping sites.

Taylorsville Lake State Park's campground is spacious.

MORE TO EXPLORE

If you are fascinated by the engineering that goes into constructing and operating dams, the Army Corps of Engineers has a visitor center on Kentucky 248 a couple of minutes north of the park entrance. Overlooking the dam, operating tower, and north end of the lake, it has an annotated diagram explaining how the dam works.

Exhibits inside the visitor center contain stuffed specimens of area wildlife, including a wild turkey and a river otter, and artifacts, including points used by the prehistoric people who hunted near the Salt River as long as 10,000 years ago.

A road off the parking lot will take you to another interesting site. The historic interpretive trail leads around several buildings moved here before their original site was flooded by the lake. They include a log cabin (circa 1840) and a one-room schoolhouse built in the mid-1800s and used as a school until 1948. For details, go to http://www.lrl.usace.army.mil/tay/.

WAVELAND STATE HISTORIC SITE

225 Waveland Museum Lane
Lexington, KY 40514
(859) 272-3611
http://www.parks.ky.gov/findparks/histparks/wl/
14 acres

THIS IS YET ANOTHER Kentucky site associated with Daniel Boone. The stately red brick, Greek revival mansion fronted by four white Corinthian columns was built between 1844 and 1848 by Boone's grandnephew Joseph Bryan.

Of the plantation's original 2,000 acres, only 14, with the mansion at their center, are preserved today. And because the main house is surrounded by gardens and important outbuildings, such as the smokehouse, icehouse, and some slave quarters, the remaining property provides a good picture of what life was like here in the years before the Civil War. But a couple of key details are missing.

The farm was located in the heart of the Bluegrass, and Joseph Bryan and his son, Joseph Henry Bryan, were highly successful horse breeders. Their stables, which are gone now but would have been built away from the house, produced champion Thoroughbreds and trotters.

Gone, too, are the acres of rolling fields in which grains and hemp were grown. Yes, hemp, *Cannabis sativa,* is the plant from which marijuana comes. But the nonhallucinogenic hemp fiber was used for making rope, sailcloth, and bags used in harvesting cotton. It was a staple crop of 19th-century Kentucky farms.

According to one account, those acres of grain waving in the breeze, amber and otherwise, conferred the name Waveland on the estate. In another account, the name came from the wavy appearance of the surrounding hills in summer haze. The version you hear during a Waveland tour depends on your guide.

Portraits of generations of Bryans hang on the mansion's walls. It and the outbuildings have been carefully furnished in period antiques, from the children's toys in the main house to the spinning wheels and kitchen utensils in the outbuildings. The house interior is light and elegant, thanks to the tall, wide windows and large, gilt-framed mirrors.

The most notable piece of furniture in this beautifully appointed setting is a true family heirloom: the small chair near the fireplace in Joseph

The ladderback chair at left, made circa 1720, may be the oldest piece of furniture in Kentucky. Now on display at Waveland State Historic Site, it came to Kentucky with Daniel Boone's family in 1779.

Bryan's office. Referred to as the Boone Chair, it was made in Pennsylvania about 1720 and traveled to North Carolina when the Boones relocated. Finally, in 1779, it was brought to the Bluegrass, and therefore is one of the oldest pieces of furniture in Kentucky.

As wonderful as it is to visit Waveland in the summer, when you can wander about the gardens and the old wood of the buildings and furniture is particularly fragrant, the Christmas Tour is quite special. The house is stunning with greenery draped throughout the rooms, usually dominated by red and gold. The guides in period costume delight in explaining to visitors that the children's stockings, stuffed with apples, oranges, and peppermints, were hung on chair backs rather than mantelpieces. A stocking hovering by the blaze could have caught fire, and the Waveland mansion could have gone up in smoke.

Waveland in winter. The Greek revival mansion was built between 1844 and 1848 by Joseph Bryan, a grandnephew of Daniel Boone.

FACILITY DETAILS

Trail: You can extend your walk though the flower and herb gardens along a 0.25-mile nature trail loop.

Other Recreation: Picnic tables and a playground are located beneath old trees on the lawn near the outbuildings.

Special Events: Christmas at Waveland (December).

MORE TO EXPLORE

The park is about six miles from central Lexington, where you can stay in the 19th-century Gratz Park Inn at the edge of the city's antebellum historic district. The 44-room federal- and Georgian-style hotel has a walled court-yard parking lot, a top-notch restaurant, and a cozy, wood-paneled bar with working fireplace. The staff insists that a friendly ghost is a permanent resident. The hotel Web site is http://www.gratzparkinn.com/.

WHITE HALL STATE HISTORIC SITE

500 White Hall Shrine Road
Richmond, KY 40475
(859) 623-9178
http://www.parks.ky.gov/findparks/histparks/wh/
13 acres

O N A CHILLY, WINDY October evening, the light is fading on the grounds of White Hall. Lights flicker behind the lace curtains in the tall, narrow windows of the opulent Italianate house. A bat circles the roof and then weaves among the branches of trees on the front lawn.

It is a Ghost Walk evening at the 44-room mansion, and the guide who leads visitors up the sidewalk to the front door cautions everyone to be quiet "so as not to disturb the spirits." The history of the house, peopled by individuals who had key roles in Kentucky history, is about to be told by the past residents. The ghosts are, in reality, costumed acting students from nearby Eastern Kentucky University.

The first stop is the parlor, where the house's owner, young Cassius Marcellus Clay, is courting his first wife, Mary Jane Warfield. It is a scene straight out of a Jane Austen novel.

Clay was an emancipationist, diplomat, newspaper publisher, and political ally of Abraham Lincoln. Cousin of Kentucky's famous statesman Henry Clay, he was a notorious firebrand, reputed to have participated in more than 200 fights and duels.

Incidents in his, his family's, and his servants' lives are re-created in the hour-long tour in which Clay himself is depicted in many stages of his long life. There is even a pistol duel on the lawn. The most affecting scene, however, does not include the master of the house. It is of a young black woman, a White Hall

During the annual Ghost Walks, an actor portrays a slave who lived at White Hall.

slave, who was accused of killing one of the Clay couple's infants. She was acquitted, and Clay eventually freed his slaves.

On the daytime, non-ghost tours of the house, conducted the rest of the year, costumed guides take visitors around White Hall and tell many stories of the owner.

The largest room is the parlor, a room just to the right of the entrance hall. When the house fell into disrepair after Clay's death, it was used to store hay. The 16-foot ceiling is supported by massive columns and decorated with ornate plaster molding. Portraits of the Russian czar and czarina, as well as other Russian paintings, appear throughout the house because Clay served as minister to Russia during Lincoln's administration and afterward.

Among Clay's accomplishments was the founding in 1845 of an antislavery newspaper, the Lexington *True American*. On exhibit on the third floor

Spirits of the past recount the history of the Clay family during the annual Ghost Walks at White Hall State Historic Site.

The Italianate mansion has 44 rooms. It was home to Cassius Marcellus Clay and his family for most of the 19th century.

of the house is a small tabletop cannon. When Clay discovered that pro-slavery sympathizers were planning to raid the paper's offices, he loaded this powerful little weapon with nails, positioned it near the entrance of the paper, and instructed his staff to fire on any invader.

In 1878, after 45 years of marriage and 10 children, Clay divorced his wife, Mary Jane. At age 84, he married Dora Richardson, a relative of one of his tenant farmers. She was 15 years old at the time. That marriage lasted a short time and also ended in divorce.

The house itself is as fascinating as its owner. Clay's father built the original portion in the Georgian style in 1798. But it was continually updated. Vents were part of its central heating system, modeled on those encountered by Clay when he was in Russia. He even installed indoor plumbing. The copper-fitted bathroom is on view during tours.

FACILITY DETAILS

Gift Shop: The shop is located in a visitor center next to the parking lot. Books detailing the life of Clay, the Lion of White Hall, are for sale, as are other books about area history. Open daily from April 1 to Labor Day. Open Wednesday–Sunday from Labor Day through October 31.

Other Recreation: There is a small picnic area with tables on the grounds and public restrooms.

Special Events: White Hall Car Show (May), Pops at the Park (August), Ghost Walk (October), Victorian Christmas (December).

MORE TO EXPLORE

One of Clay's daughters, Laura, was active in the women's suffrage movement and, after women won the right to vote, was the first woman nominated for president of the United States by a major party (the Democrats, in 1920). She never married, and she supported herself by managing a 300-acre farm, leased from her father, which she owned after his death. You can visit her gravesite in the Lexington Cemetery, where many other famous Kentuckians are buried, including Henry Clay, Mary Breckinridge, John Hunt Morgan, and Adolph Rupp. For directions and monument locations, go to http://www.lexcem.org/.

WILLIAM WHITLEY HOUSE
STATE HISTORIC SITE

625 William Whitley Road
Stanford, KY 40484-9770
606-355-2881
http://www.parks.ky.gov/findparks/histparks/ww/
40 acres

IN THE LAST QUARTER of the 18th century, many explorers and settlers arrived in Kentucky through the Cumberland Gap, traveling westward along the Wilderness Road. The threat of attack by American Indians (not to mention bears, poisonous snakes, and other frontier wildlife) was very real, so many of these newcomers headed to fortified settlements, such as Harrodsburg and Boonesborough.

When William and Esther Whitley and their daughters moved to Kentucky from Virginia in the 1770s, they too traveled through the Cumberland Gap and along the Wilderness Road. Unlike many other settlers, however, they acquired 10 acres along this frontier route and eventually replaced a log cabin with an elegant Georgian mansion.

At first glance, Sportsman's Hill, as Whitley named it, looks strangely out of place perched on a small summit surrounded by mature walnuts, oaks, and catalpa trees. This was a dangerous frontier, and the Whitley property, reachable by a series of secondary roads, still feels isolated. Many aspects of the house, finished in 1794, reflect its dual role as home and fortification. Its visitors, including Daniel Boone and George Rogers Clark, knew it as the Guardian of the Wilderness Road.

A young reenactor checks his pennywhistle during a semiannual Kentucky Militia Living History Encampment at William Whitley House State Historic Site.

The William Whitley House, completed in 1794, was the first brick home in Kentucky. Note the owner's initials in the patterned brick.

Notice that the front door seems unusually high off the ground. It is reached by a series of steep steps that were not added until much later. Originally, the family got to the door by climbing a ladder they pulled in behind them. Windows look symmetrical from the front, but as another defense from American Indians' attacks, interior walls end in the middle of many of them. The house also has a secret staircase and a windowless kitchen with a false ceiling, providing a cramped but secure hiding place.

Lesser individuals might have felt worn down by what must have been a siege mentality, a constant vigilance. By all accounts, though, the Whitleys were made of stern stuff. Whitley made his reputation as a fighter who organized Kentucky militia troops to launch counterattacks on warring American Indians after raids. Esther did the same when William was away. She, too, was reportedly a crack shot.

Even in the face of the dangers of the frontier, Sportsman's Hill was a center of social activity. The Whitleys entertained in their parlor, one wall of which is paneled in elaborately carved black walnut. There is a large fireplace that must have provided a cozy focal point for wintertime gatherings. Skilled craftsmen left their marks all over the house. Eagles are carved into the staircase. The brick exterior, in the Flemish bond pattern, features the initials WW over the front door and EW over the back. This was among the first houses west of the Appalachians to be built of brick.

The name of the house comes from Whitley's love of sports of all kinds, horse racing in particular. In many ways, American racing began here. Looking out a window in the front of the house, you will see a field across the road. It is not part of the state's historic site property, but it was the location of Whitley's racecourse.

Instead of using turf, as was common in Europe, Whitley built his circular track with a clay surface. And perhaps because he was being patriotically anti-British, Whitley ordained that the races at Sportsman's Hill be run counterclockwise, the opposite of races in England.

The autumn meets became fixtures of the region, and elaborate breakfasts were served in the mansion at the conclusion of the early morning races. In addition to familiar fare such as roast turkey with cranberry sauce, leg of bear often turned up on the menu.

The children's bedroom.

By the turn of the century, the Cherokee hostilities in Kentucky were a matter of history, and the Whitleys, who had acquired more land to expand their estate, settled into farming, entertaining, and raising their 11 children. But William Whitley was not finished fighting American Indians.

When the War of 1812 broke out, Governor Isaac Shelby called for volunteers, and the 64-year-old Whitley joined up. He was killed in the Battle of the Thames, near Detroit, in which the famous Shawnee chief Tecumseh was also killed while leading his warriors in the service of the British. In 1818, the Kentucky legislature named Whitley County in honor of William Whitley's services to the commonwealth.

FACILITY DETAILS

Museum: Sportsman's Hill is furnished in period antiques as a historic home museum. Guided tours are offered April through October with limited winter hours based on weather. Call ahead to make sure the house will be open. There is a fee for tours.

Gift Shop: The house contains a gift shop at the side entrance where tours begin. The selection of books is mainly about Kentucky history.

Recreation: Ten acres of the site are set aside with two picnic shelters and a playground. Shelters are available for group rental.

Special Events: Kentucky Militia Living History Encampments and Whitley House Reenactors (September, October), Sportsman's Hill Antique Car/Truck Show (September).

MORE TO EXPLORE

The 780-acre Cedar Creek Lake is only a short drive from the William Whitley House. Anglers can try their luck in catching bluegill, crappie, largemouth bass, and others among the half-million fish with which the lake is stocked.

SOUTH CENTRAL
KENTUCKY PARKS

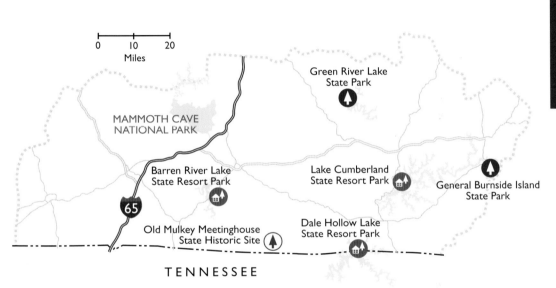

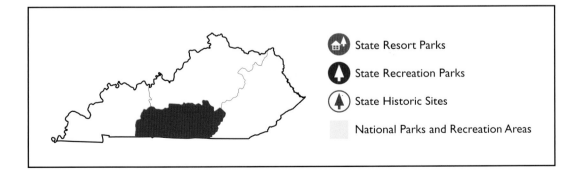

State Resort Parks

State Recreation Parks

State Historic Sites

National Parks and Recreation Areas

SOUTH CENTRAL
STATE PARKS

- Year-round
- Seasonal

		Park Acres	Lake Acres	Lodge and Dining Room	Cottages	Campground	✈ : Airport; ▲ : Air Camp
RESORT PARKS							
Barren River Lake	Lucas	1,053	10,000	•	•	•	
Dale Hollow Lake	Burkesville	3,398	27,700	•		○	
Lake Cumberland	Jamestown	3,117	50,250	•	•	○	
RECREATIONAL PARKS							
General Burnside	Burnside	430	50,250			○	
Green River Lake	Campbellsville	1,331	8,200			○	
HISTORIC SITES							
Old Mulkey Meetinghouse	Tompkinsville	79					

Golf (18-Hole, 9-Hole, or D: Disc Course)	Marina (L: Boat Launch Only)	Rental Boats	Swimming (P: Outdoor Pool, I: Indoor Pool, S: Slide, B: Beach)	Trails (Miles)	Riding Stables (⟳: Equestrian Trails)	Mountain Biking	Tennis Courts	Miniature Golf	Playgrounds	Picnic Area	Museum or Nature Center	Recreation/Interpretation Program
18	○	●	P/B	4	○	●	●		●	●		●
18	●	●	P	15	⟳	●			●	●		●
D	○	○	P/I	5.6	○		●	○	●	●	○	●
18	●	●		0.25					●	●		○
	L	B		28		●		○	●	●		○
									●	●		

79

BARREN RIVER LAKE STATE RESORT PARK

1149 State Park Road
Lucas, KY 42156
(270) 646-2151 or (800) 325-0057
http://www.parks.ky.gov/findparks/resortparks/br/
1,053 acres; 10,000 lake acres

THE BARRENS REGION of south central Kentucky got its name when the early settlers encountered vast stretches of tall grasslands (in other words, prairie) that extended over this part of the state. Since it was not covered in the dense woodlands to which they were accustomed, they assumed the soil was barren.

Far from being unproductive, the land was being managed by the resident American Indians, who preserved the prairie by regularly burning it. This practice maintained the grasslands for the herds of bison and elk on which they depended for food and hides. Today, the importance of agriculture in the region certainly demonstrates the inherent richness of the soil.

The wildlife at Barren River Lake State Resort Park is on a much more modest scale than bison and elk, though white-tailed deer are abundant. Keep your eyes peeled around your accommodation if you are staying at one of the lakefront beach cottages. You may glimpse a handsome little fence lizard (the male has a bright blue throat patch) darting up and down the exterior walls. Groundhogs are especially fond of the road culverts near the golf course. And at night in the summertime, you may hear the distinctive, haunting call of the chuck-will's-widow (a close relative of the whippoor-will) just after sunset.

In contrast to many of the state's other resort parks, Barren River Lake is, appropriately, much less wooded and more open. Contemporary lodge rooms and cottages have tall windows that let in lots of sunlight. The lake, taking up almost 10 times the area of the parkland tucked alongside its eastern shore, dominates the park.

While it is certainly possible to spend quiet time here reading or socializing with friends in the spacious cottages or lodge rooms, Barren River Lake is a park for visitors interested in activity. There is a paved trail for bikers, as well as a couple of hiking trails. You can swim in the pool or at the beach. A marina serves boaters and anglers. And the park has an 18-hole golf course, as well as playgrounds and game courts.

The native grasses prairie on the west shore of Barren River Lake is maintained by the U.S. Army Corps of Engineers. The tall flower is moth mullein.

A bench near the lodge overlooks Barren River Lake.

Members of the Clan of the Wolf engage in a round of throwing stones during the Glasgow Highland Games.

The annual Glasgow Highland Games, held around Memorial Day weekend, is the park's signature event. Located only 11 miles from Glasgow, Barren River Lake State Resort Park is the logical choice as the venue for this celebration of the region's Scottish settler heritage. Normally empty fields near the golf course, as well as the park's campground, are turned into reasonable facsimiles of 18th-century Highlands villages. Bagpipe and fiddle music fills the air. Men stride around in kilts. Women stir iron kettles of savory stews.

The festival organizers get a real Scottish laird to travel from the old

Anglers at sunset on Barren River Lake.

country to be chief of the games. He presides over such traditional tests of strength as caber tossing, hammer throwing, and Highland wrestling. In case your closet is missing a kilt in your ancestral tartan, vendors sell reasonably authentic Celtic wares. And you may even spot someone dressed in a blend of American Indian and Scottish costume. There is a historical connection. Ask one of the games goers so attired, and he will obligingly explain it to you at length.

For details about each year's festival, which includes concerts by contemporary Celtic rock bands as well as Lunch with the Chief and the Grand Banquet and Tartan Ball, go to http://www.glasgowhighlandgames.com/.

FACILITY DETAILS

Lodge: The Louie B. Nunn Lodge is named in honor of the late Barren County native and Glasgow attorney who was Kentucky's governor from 1967 to 1971. It has 51 rooms, many with lake views, and the 146-seat Driftwood Restaurant, with two walls of windows overlooking the water. There

SOUTH CENTRAL

Friends relax by the lodge swimming pool at Barren River Lake State Resort Park.

are many common areas in the lodge with comfortable sofas and chairs. A landing above the lobby check-in desk has tables and chairs so that it is a quiet place for a small meeting or a game of cards.

Cottages: There are two groups of these, each with two bedrooms. They can sleep up to 8 or 10. The lodge-vicinity cottages are set among trees. The very spacious beach cottages are near the lake and have large, gas-operated fireplaces. Screened porches with lake views are perfect for al fresco yet mosquito-free dining.

Campground: The campground, reached by taking the first left turn after entering the park, has 99 sites with utilities hookups, two bathhouses, a playground, a volleyball court, and a boat ramp exclusively for campers' use.

Trails: There are three trails. The 1-mile Connell Nature Trail makes a loop that begins near an old springhouse and passes between the beach cottages and the beach. You may very well spot a deer or six as you cross a grassy field between wooded portions of the path. The Lena Madesin Phillips Trail is 0.5 mile long and has interpretive signs about both the history and nature of the park. The paved Bike and Hiking Trail is the park's longest at 2.5 miles. It winds along the main park road and through the back nine of the golf course.

Fishing and Boating: The park's marina has slips for about 100 boats. You can keep your own here for a fee or rent one. The primary activity is fishing. Species you are likely to catch here include bluegill, channel catfish, crappie, rough fish, and largemouth, white, and hybrid striped bass.

Swimming: The lodge has a swimming pool and wading pool overlooking the lake. The sandy beach south of the lodge has bathhouse facilities.

Golf Course: Most of the front 9 holes of the 18-hole course are located on a peninsula, so your play is surrounded by water. Clubs are available to rent, as are carts.

Other Recreation: Tennis courts, a basketball court, picnic shelters, horse-back riding stables, five playgrounds, and a sand volleyball court.

Special Events: Buffalo Night (February), Glasgow Highland Games (May), Youth Fishing Derby (June), Fourth of July Fireworks, Spookout Weekend (October), Geocaching Weekend (October).

MORE TO EXPLORE

The park is near Kentucky's famous cave country, which includes Mammoth Cave National Park. For an excellent introduction to the geology and cultural and natural history of caves, visit the American Cave Museum in Horse Cave, a town literally built on top of Hidden River Cave. It is about 25 miles from the park. For information, go to http://www.cavern.org/ or call (270) 786-1466.

DALE HOLLOW LAKE STATE RESORT PARK

6371 State Park Road
Burkesville, KY 42717
(270) 433-7431 or (800) 325-2282
http://www.parks.ky.gov/findparks/resortparks/dh/
3,398 acres; 27,700 lake acres

THE THREE-STORY GLASS and limestone lodge at Dale Hollow State Resort Park is perched on a cliff hundreds of feet above the surface of the lake. From the water, especially at dusk, when electric light shines from its tall windows, the lodge looks like a futuristic castle standing guard over the islands beneath it.

You will find that the view of the water from those tall windows is wonderful, too. The dining room has floor-to-ceiling plate glass on three sides and a 37-foot-tall stone fireplace. Each light-filled room has a private balcony with lake views.

The lodge features excellent accommodation in one of the most contemporary designs in the parks system, but you may prefer to explore Dale Hollow Lake from the comfort of a houseboat. With more than 40 square miles of water and 650 miles of shoreline, it has seemingly countless inlets and coves you can float into and claim as your own for a few days. Tie up for the night, swim in the lake, and fall asleep to the woodland chorus of the multiple frog species that chirp and buzz after sundown.

The park is on the southern border of Kentucky, so much of the lake and portions of the larger islands you see from the lodge are in Tennessee. I once went houseboating with friends here, and every time we passed back into Kentucky from Tennessee, our patriotic Captain Ellen insisted we all stand and sing "My Old Kentucky Home."

The clear water and numerous inlets are also popular with anglers, both human and avian. Great blue herons are common. Dale Hollow Lake is one of the places in Kentucky where American bald eagles spend the winter.

Landlubbers will find much to do here, too. The park has about 15 miles of multiuse trails. If you bring your horse, there are some horse camping sites. If your visit time is limited, one of the most rewarding trails in the park system is the Eagle Point Trail, which winds gently, with just a couple of short and steep parts, to a bluff giving a view of the lodge to the right and of the lake and its islands straight ahead and to the left.

Facing page:
View of the
Mary Ray Oaken
Lodge from
the Eagle Point
Lookout.

Courting wild turkeys on the golf course are oblivious of nearby humans.

You will notice a cluster of buildings, including an A-frame house, on Trooper Island. This is a camp operated by the Kentucky State Police that is used both as a scuba training facility for the troopers and as a summer camp for at-risk children.

Dale Hollow Lake State Resort Park's very scenic golf course, with combined vistas of mountains and water, attracts players from Bowling Green and beyond. Even so, it deserves to be busier. Keep an eye out in the tall grass by the fairways, where wild turkey commonly feed. They often wander onto the manicured grass, which is apparently a favorite mating ground for them.

FACILITY DETAILS

Lodge: The Mary Ray Oaken Lodge has 60 guestrooms. If the weather is fine, have an al fresco breakfast on one of the stone-walled patios outside the dining room overlooking the lake. The park gift shop is located off the lobby. Conference facilities accommodate as many as 250 people.

Campground: The 145-site campground is set in deep woods. All sites have utilities hookups. Two dozen sites are equipped for horse camping. In addition to the usual service buildings, the campground has a small amphitheater and its own swimming pool. There are also four primitive cabins (no plumbing), which can be rented. Bring your own bedding. Open from mid-March to mid-November.

Trails: Boles Hollow and Campers Path (each 0.2 mile long) are open to foot traffic only. The other 14.6 miles of trails, many tracing former logging roads, reach into every corner of the park and are open to hikers, mountain bikers, and horses. Do not try to take short cuts between trails. They are separated by hollows with very steep sides and rugged terrain.

Cave: Guided tours and exploration by permit are available in Cindy Cave, located approximately at the geographic center of the park. Bats, cave crick-

Horses are welcome on the Eagle Point Trail overlooking Dale Hollow Lake.

ets, crayfish, and salamanders are among the residents. You can rent caving gear at the lodge desk.

Fishing and Boating: Dale Hollow Lake has yielded a big one that did not get away: the world-record smallmouth bass (1 ounce short of 12 pounds) was caught here. Other fish include bluegill, crappie, muskie, rainbow trout, and white bass. The park has a marina with a snack bar, dock, boat ramp, and 200 boat slips. Pontoon boats and fishing boats can be rented by the day. Privately owned marinas outside the park rent houseboats.

Golf Course: In addition to being X rated thanks to the amorous turkeys, the 18-hole championship golf course has been nationally ranked by *Golf Digest*. The design includes bentgrass tees and greens and zoysia fairways. It is very hilly, and its landscape challenges include springs, ponds, small caves, and numerous rock outcroppings. A new clubhouse, pro shop, and practice range opened in 2007.

Other Recreation: Picnic areas and playgrounds are located within the park, and various activities are scheduled in the summer.

Special Events: Eagle Watch Weekends (January–February), Road Rally (March), Geocache Weekend (April), Kids Fishing Derby (June), Dale Hollow 5-K Classic (August), Horsemen's Reunion (October), Beginning Caving Expedition (November).

MORE TO EXPLORE

The park is almost an hour and a half's drive from I-65, the closest interstate highway, so it takes some patience to get here. Luckily, there are many signs along the winding route that point the way.

A curious historical note: Close to the park, in Cumberland County, one of the first oil discoveries in the United States was made in 1829. Briny springs in the area were a source of salt; a well being drilled in search of saltwater hit oil instead, sending an impressive black geyser shooting into the air.

GENERAL BURNSIDE STATE PARK

8801 South Highway 27
Burnside, KY 42519
(606) 561-4104 or (606) 561-4192
http://www.parks.ky.gov/findparks/recparks/ge/
430 acres; 50,250 lake acres

IF YOU HAVE ever had a fantasy about shutting yourself off from the world with the aid of a moat, consider camping at this park. A causeway from U.S. 27 crosses over the water of Lake Cumberland to Kentucky's only state park located entirely on an island. General Burnside State Park is situated at the far eastern end of the lake. A walk to the edge of its wooded bluffs will give you commanding views across the water and of the nearby mountains.

And if the name Burnside is ringing a bell, you might be the proud possessor of a bushy set of side-whiskers. This entry from *A Dictionary of Eponyms* by Cyril Leslie Beeching (Oxford University Press) reveals all:

> Ambrose Everett Burnside (1824–81) was one of the least distinguished generals of the American Civil War—on either side of the conflict. Yet, with the exception of the redoubtable "Stonewall" Jackson, he is the only one to have given his name to the English language. Burnside was

Relaxing after a cookout in the campground.

91

Dogwood in bloom in the campground at General Burnside State Park.

the commander of the Army of the Potomac in 1862, but his lack of success in the Fredericksburg campaign led to his dismissal the following year. Under General Grant, he again failed to prove his ability on the field of battle, and his conduct was criticized by a court of enquiry. He resigned his commission in 1865 and went into politics. General Burnside is in fact remembered for his distinguished side-whiskers—which he gave his name to as burnsides, or sideburns—rather than his somewhat undistinguished military career.

Why is a Kentucky park named after the general? His troops patrolled the Cumberland River and had a lookout post near what is the current island. Burnside was also the officer to accept the surrender of Confederate forces at Cumberland Gap, which was probably the high point of his service.

FACILITY DETAILS

Campground: This is a hilly, heavily wooded campground. The landscape gives many sites here more privacy than those at other campgrounds in the park system. The 94 sites have utilities hookups, and there are two central service buildings with showers and restrooms. Open from mid-March to mid-November.

Trails: A short, rocky trail winds from the back of campsite 26 to an overlook on the north end of the island. It has a view of Lake Cumberland and a bridge carrying traffic on Kentucky 90.

Fishing and Boating: A marina next to the park has boat slips, rental fishing boats, ski boats, pontoon boats, and houseboats. The park has a six-lane launching ramp. Lake Cumberland fish include crappie and various bass species (largemouth, smallmouth, and striped).

Golf Course: The park's 18-hole golf course, which takes up most of the island's acreage, underwent a complete renovation beginning in October

Setting up a tent in the wooded campgrounds.

SOUTH CENTRAL

2006 and reopened in May 2008. Brian Ault, architect of both the Dale Hollow Lake and Grayson Lake parks' courses, was responsible for the design. In addition to a fully equipped pro shop, the new course has a driving range.

Other Recreation: Picnic shelters and tables, a playground, and a volleyball court are located on the island.

MORE TO EXPLORE

The park is about 25 miles from the Big South Fork Scenic Railway in Stearns, which features a scenic, 16-mile, three-hour train trip through parts of the Daniel Boone National Forest and the Big South Fork National River and Recreation Area. The excursion includes a stop at the historic Blue Heron Coal Mining Camp. The train, which has both open and closed passenger cars, travels a century-old route through mountain ravines and along cliffs and streams. For more information, go to http://www.bsfsry.com/.

GREEN RIVER LAKE STATE PARK

179 Park Office Road
Campbellsville, KY 42718
(270) 465-8255
http://www.parks.ky.gov/findparks/recparks/gr/
1,331 acres; 8,200 lake acres

DAWN ON A HOT SUMMER DAY finds the campers at Green River Lake State Park waking to a golden sunrise, light painting the dense trees on the hills around the lake and casting glowing ripples on the water. The youngsters are the first to be up and about. They pedal all sizes of bicycles through the narrow lanes of the campground, past small tents and large RVs. Some are a bit wobbly. Others streak toward their destinations as though they are in the Tour de France. You can tell that they want to squeeze every drop of time out of the day.

Some abandon their bikes for playground swings. Other girls and boys have brought their fishing poles to the water's edge, hoping to make the first catch of the morning. Meanwhile, the grownups are finally stirring, and the smell of sizzling bacon floats through the air.

The waterside campground at Green River Lake State Park.

A sunset swing in the playground.

Green River Lake State Park's campground, situated on the edge of the lake, is the most popular and the busiest in the state's system. It is easy to see why. The view from the campground is not simply of an unrelieved expanse of water. Wooded hills rise from the shorelines, and successive spits of land create a maze of channels. You will long for a boat so you can go exploring to find out what is on the other side of this or that peninsula.

To reach the campground, you have to drive straight through the park. Except for the frequent spotting of bluebirds, you may not appreciate the other main attraction of Green River Lake State Park. There are 28 miles of trails here. All are open to walkers. Mountain bikers and horseback riders use long stretches of many, too. The trails loop and cross through hills, woods, and meadows. It will take more than one visit, or an extended stay, to travel them all.

The park's marina is privately operated and has a couple of unique attractions. First are the floating cabins, one- and two-story frame structures built on a pier stretching along the lake, parallel to the shore. You can tie your boat up at the back of a cabin and use this as your base of operations for exploring the lake.

Second are the pet fish. Green River–style catfish, fried in a peppery batter, is a local delicacy. But you will not find the finny friends at the marina on the menu. Dozens of them come to one of the docks to feed on bread the staff and visitors toss into the water. Some will even eat out of your hand. Never had your fingers nibbled on by a catfish? You have not lived. Give it a try.

FACILITY DETAILS

Campground: The 157-site campground, right on the water, has a grocery and three service buildings with showers, restrooms, and washers and driers. The park gift shop is next to the campground, which is open mid-March to mid-November.

Floating Cabins: A private company, not the state, operates these. For information on rates and availability, call (800) 488-2512 or visit http://www.greenrivermarina.com/.

Trails: Three main trails loop through the park, with many spur trails shooting off from the larger ones. When the trail map advises that the terrain is difficult, take it seriously. Some of the paths are quite rocky and steep, so bring your toughest hiking boots. The Marina Main Trail, which takes you along the lake, makes for a wonderful dawn or dusk hike. Watch out for mountain bikers, though.

Fishing and Boating: A boat ramp is located at the campground. The marina, down the road from the main park entrance, has 200 covered slips. You can rent houseboats, fishing boats, ski boats, jet skis, and pontoon boats. Open March–November. The marina telephone number is (800) 488-2512. If you cannot take a boat onto the lake, you can cast from a fishing pier at the campground. In addition to the non-pet catfish, there are white, largemouth, smallmouth, and Kentucky bass, bluegill, crappie, and muskie.

Other Recreation: An 18-hole miniature golf course is located at the campground, as are playgrounds, picnic tables and shelter, a basketball court, a volleyball court, and a sandy beach. Swimming in the lake is permitted

A mallard duck keeps watch over the floating cabins at the marina.

from the beach. Green River Stables, where you can hire a horse, is located next to the park; call (270) 789-4525 for information.

Special Events: Trick or Trot (October), 5-K Run or Walk (October).

MORE TO EXPLORE

The dividing line between the eastern and central time zones passes through Green River Lake. The park is in the eastern time zone, but the Lake Cumberland area, which is east of Green River, is in the central time zone. Confused yet? Just be aware that you might want to call ahead to a restaurant or other attraction to make sure you are arriving between opening and closing times.

LAKE CUMBERLAND
STATE RESORT PARK

5465 State Park Road
Jamestown, KY 42629
(270) 343-3111 or (800) 325-1709
http://www.parks.ky.gov/findparks/resortparks/lc/
3,117 acres; 50,250 lake acres

IT WAS a very quiet, early summer morning at Lake Cumberland. The weekend crowds had left, and the wooded circle of two-story, chalet-style cottages overlooking the lake was deserted. Walking around the building from the wooden deck of one of the Wildwood Cottages, I was startled to see a tiny, spotted fawn tumbling down the slope of the mound at the center of the cottage circle. Legs flailing in all directions, it rolled to a stop. Its fur still shining wet, this little deer had just arrived in the world. Another sound of an animal crashing through nearby trees meant that Mama had taken off into the woods when I intruded on the scene. And even though

A newborn fawn rests in the leaves near the Wildwood Cottages.

she was gone for the moment, the newborn was going to be just fine. I left immediately, had a late breakfast at the park lodge, and returned a couple of hours later to find the doe attending her baby.

Another uncharacteristic aspect of my stop at Lake Cumberland State Resort Park was that the lake level had been greatly lowered by the Army Corps of Engineers. (Several months earlier, they had discovered that the Wolf Creek Dam impounding the lake needed extensive repairs.) In many places along the shoreline, 30 or more feet of rock were exposed, and the lake surface was reduced by more than 13,000 acres. Of, course, if you are an angler, this concentrates the fish population density and increases your odds of landing a catch! The lake level will be in flux for a while; this is a major engineering project. But that does not detract from a whole host of activities at the park.

Lake Cumberland has one of two 18-hole disc golf (also known as Frisbee golf) courses in the state parks system. It is laid out near the main lodge. You can also hike two scenic trails or, in season, explore the wooded terrain on a horse hired from the park's stables. The forests are the typical oak, hickory, and beech woods found in this part of Kentucky, crowded with wildflowers in the spring and bright with colors in the fall. Walk them in the middle of the week and you will encounter more white-tailed deer than humans, not to mention a variety of woodland songbirds, woodpeckers, and hawks.

One reason the park is so rich in wildlife and so peaceful is that it is located on a peninsula. The landscape is hilly, too, so whether you are staying in a cottage, one of the two lodges, or the campground, you will feel surrounded by nature and insulated from other park visitors. The raccoons and skunks you will frequently see strolling casually around the park accommodations with a distinctly proprietary air enhance this impression.

FACILITY DETAILS

Lodges: The 63-room Lure Lodge has a climate-controlled, indoor pool complex for year-round swimming. The complex includes a game room, exercise room, and hot tub. The dining room overlooks the lake, but most of the rooms have woodland views. The park's gift shop is in the Lure Lodge. The smaller Pumpkin Creek Lodge, with 13 rooms, feels like a boutique hotel and has a series of patios and porches. Three rooms look onto the water.

Facing page: Anglers try their fishing luck off Cumberland Point.

Playing checkers
in the Lure
Lodge recreation
room at Lake
Cumberland
State Resort
Park.

Cottages: There are 19 one- and two-bedroom cottages in two waterside locations of the park. In addition, there are the two-story Wildwood Cottages. These have working fireplaces.

Campground: The park's 146 wooded sites all have utilities hookups. Service buildings include showers, restrooms, and laundry. Open mid-March through November.

Country Store: At a small convenience store by the main park road, you can rent clubs and balls for the miniature golf course next to it. A second, outdoor swimming pool is located just behind the store. Open seasonally.

Trails: The Lake Bluff Trail has a total length of about 4 miles. If you can manage the whole distance, you will get a thorough tour of the park, since it passes through woods, beside the lake, and near several of the buildings. It crosses park roads at several points, so you can also choose shorter walks. The terrain along the 1.6-mile Baugh Branch Trail is pretty steep and rugged. You will encounter fewer fellow hikers on this one, but perhaps more wildlife.

Fishing and Boating: Sport fish include largemouth, smallmouth, white, and Kentucky bass, bluegill, crappie, rockfish, and walleye. The marina has 100 open boat slips, and you can rent fishing boats, pontoon boats, houseboats, and ski boats. Several commercial marinas serve Lake Cumberland, too. The park marina is open April through October. Go to http://www.statedock.com/ or call (888) 782-8336.

Disc Golf Course: The 9-hole traditional golf course was converted to an 18-hole disc course in 2007. For more information about the game, visit the Web site of the Professional Disc Golf Association, http://www.pdga.com/.

Other Recreation: Other seasonal activities include a riding stable, planned recreation, tennis, volleyball, and shuffleboard. Picnic tables and playgrounds are found in several locations.

Special Events: Buffalo Dinner (January), Geocache Weekend (April).

MORE TO EXPLORE

The million or so brown and rainbow trout stocked in all of Kentucky's lakes, including Lake Cumberland, are raised at the Wolf Creek National Fish Hatchery in Jamestown. The hatchery has an excellent visitor and environmental education center that includes exhibits about Kentucky's ecosystems, as well as large aquariums filled with fish found in the state's lakes. It is a fascinating stop for children and adults alike. For details, go to http://www.fws.gov/wolfcreek/.

OLD MULKEY MEETINGHOUSE STATE HISTORIC SITE

38 Old Mulkey Park Road
Tompkinsville, KY 42167-8766
(270) 487-8481
http://www.parks.ky.gov/findparks/histparks/om/
79 acres

AT FIRST GLANCE, the Old Mulkey Meetinghouse appears to be an oversize log cabin or perhaps a small log barn. But look more carefully. The design contains important Christian symbolism. It may not be as grand as Notre Dame or Westminster Abbey, but the devout of frontier Kentucky honored the architectural conventions of church building as best they could with the materials they had.

Notice that a little bit of the wall sticks out on both of the long sides of the building. It is subtle, but the resulting shape of the meetinghouse is that of a cross. Notice, too, that there are three doors, to symbolize the Holy Trinity.

There is no stained glass, but there are large windows to let in daylight. These could be closed against the elements with wooden shutters. The floor is made of short wood planks.

When it was built in 1804, Old Mulkey was called the Mill Creek Baptist Church. Settlers from the Carolinas, led by Philip Mulkey, formed the core of the first congregation, whose first pastor was John Mulkey. One of its members was Hannah Boone Pennington, frontiersman Daniel Boone's sister. Her cenotaph is among the dozens of memorial stones found in the cemetery just north of the church; look for the headstone with a carving of an angel in profile. Others interred here include many men who were soldiers in the Revolutionary War.

The Second Great Awakening, a Protestant reform movement in the late 18th and early 19th centuries, included revivalist camp meetings to which thousands of people would travel to hear the most eloquent preachers of the day deliver sermons. Families arrived with enough food to last for many days or weeks, so it is perfectly appropriate that today's park contains a couple of picnic areas.

By 1809, the reform movement caused a schism in the Mill Creek congregation. (Or perhaps the backless, peg-legged benches everyone had to sit on for several hours every Sunday morning had their effect.) Those who

The Old Mulkey Meetinghouse is the oldest log meetinghouse in Kentucky. Hannah Boone Pennington, Daniel Boone's sister, was one of the members; her grave is nearby.

broke away from Mulkey's flock started a new Mill Creek Baptist Church. The original was then called the Mulkey Meetinghouse, and the flavor of Christianity favored by Mulkey and his followers eventually grew into the Church of Christ denomination.

The state park grounds are striking for being heavily wooded. The surrounding Monroe County countryside is rolling farmland consisting of cattle pastures and corn, soybean, and hay fields. If you visit at twilight, the electric lights in the empty meetinghouse glow warmly but a little eerily. The worn headstones nearby probably contribute to that effect.

The park has no hiking trails, but there is a path from the west side of the graveyard that leads through the woods. It winds past a lone monument, situated incongruously on the floor of the tall hickory and oak forest that has grown up on what was once a homestead. The carving in the stone identifies this as the grave of two of Confederate general Stonewall Jackson's cousins.

FACILITY DETAILS

Gift Shop: The shop stocks books on the history of the Old Mulkey Meetinghouse as well as a selection of Kentucky-made crafts and candies.

Recreation: There are two picnic sites. One has a covered shelter, which can be rented for groups, and playground equipment. The other consists of tables in a tree-shaded area. The path to the Jackson family grave is 0.1 mile long.

Special Events: A handful of annual events include a cornhole tournament (October) and a Halloween celebration (October).

MORE TO EXPLORE

If you are interested in the history of the frontier in this part of the state, known as the Barrens, visit the South Central Kentucky Cultural Center in Glasgow, about 45 minutes' drive from the historic site. It has many exhibits on pioneer life in the region. The museum's Web site is http://www.cityofglasgow.org/sckcc/.

EASTERN
KENTUCKY PARKS

OHIO

Greenbo Lake
State Resort Park

Carter Caves
State Resort Park

WEST
VIRGINIA

Grayson Lake
State Park

64

Yatesville Lake
State Park

Paintsville Lake
State Park

RED RIVER
GORGE

Natural Bridge
State Resort Park

Jenny Wiley
State Resort Park

Fishtrap Lake
State Park

Buckhorn Lake
State Resort Park

75

Carr Creek
State Park

VIRGINIA

Levi Jackson
Wilderness Road
State Park

Kingdom Come
State Park

Dr. Thomas Walker
State Historic Site

0   10   20
Miles

Cumberland Falls
State Resort Park

Pine Mountain
State Resort Park

CUMBERLAND GAP
NATIONAL HISTORIC PARK

BIG SOUTH FORK
NATIONAL RIVER
& RECREATION AREA

TENNESSEE

EASTERN

	State Resort Parks
	State Recreation Parks
	State Historic Sites
	National Parks and Recreation Areas

EASTERN
STATE PARKS

- Year-round
○ Seasonal

		Park Acres	Lake Acres	Lodge and Dining Room	Cottages	Campground	✈: Airport; ▲: Air Camp
RESORT PARKS							
Buckhorn Lake	Buckhorn	856	1,200	●	●		
Carter Caves	Olive Hill	2,000	45	●	●	○	
Cumberland Falls	Corbin	1,776		●	●	○	
Greenbo Lake	Greenup	3,008	225	●		○	
Jenny Wiley	Prestonsburg	1,498	1,150	●	●	○	
Natural Bridge	Slade	2,250	60	●	●	○	
Pine Mountain	Pineville	1,519		●	●		
RECREATIONAL PARKS							
Carr Creek	Sassafras	29	750			○	
Fishtrap Lake	Pikeville	300	1,071				
Grayson Lake	Olive Hill	1,512	1,500			○	
Kingdom Come	Cumberland	1,283	3.5			●	
Levi Jackson Wilderness Road	London	896				●	
Paintsville Lake	Staffordsville	242	1,139			●	
Yatesville Lake	Louisa	808	2,300			○	
HISTORIC SITES							
Dr. Thomas Walker	Barbourville	12					

EASTERN

Golf (18-Hole, 9-Hole, or D: Disc Course)	Marina (L: Boat Launch Only)	Rental Boats	Swimming (P: Outdoor Pool, I: Indoor Pool, S: Slide, B: Beach)	Trails (Miles)	Riding Stables (U: Equestrian Trails)	Mountain Biking	Tennis Courts	Miniature Golf	Playgrounds	Picnic Area	Museum or Nature Center	Recreation/Interpretation Program
	○	○	P/B	2			●	○	●	●		●
9	○	○	P	26	○ U	●	●	○	●	●		●
			P	20	○ U		●		●	●	●	●
	○	○	P/S	25+	U	●	●	○	●	●		●
D	L	○	P	13		●			●	●	●	●
		○	P	20				○	●	●	●	●
18			P	11		●		○	●	●	●	●
			B						●	●		
	○		P/S	2.3					●	●		
18	L		B	3.8					●	●		○
		○		5				○	○	○	●	●
			P/S	8.5				○	●	●	○	○
	○	○							●	●		
18	●	○	B	20+	U	●			●	●		
								○	●	●		

BUCKHORN LAKE STATE RESORT PARK

4441 Kentucky Highway 1833
Buckhorn, KY 41721
(606) 398-7510 or (800) 325-0058
http://www.parks.ky.gov/findparks/resortparks/bk/
856 acres; 1,200 lake acres

Tucked away deep in the Appalachians, Buckhorn Lake State Resort Park takes some determination to reach. Your car will crawl up winding, two-lane roads after the relative speed of the Mountain Parkway. Once you finally gain the park entrance after a surprisingly sudden turn off Kentucky 1833, the road leading to the lodge seems endless, too. But use the drive to relax and begin to take in the park's features.

Tall, rocky cliffs line one side of the route. If you come here in May, you will see dust mop–shaped bundles of tiny white flowers growing out of the mountainside. This is false goat's beard (*Astilbe biternata*), a characteristic plant of the Cumberland Plateau, but one you will not often spy from a car.

Wildflower spotting is one of the seasonal pleasures of Buckhorn in spring and early summer. The distinctive, vase-shaped jack-in-the-pulpit

The crowd stakes out waterfront viewing places for the Fourth of July fireworks at Buckhorn Lake State Resort Park.

Fourth of July fireworks explode over the lodge.

(*Arisaema triphyllum*) can also be seen in May. It grows along the stream bank on the 1.5-mile Moonshiner's Hollow Trail. Tulip poplar trees are flowering then, too, and a brochure you can get at the front desk of the lodge will guide you to other trees and plants of the woods here, including oaks, beeches, ironwood, serviceberry, and dogwood.

The mixed hardwood forest provides lots of color in the fall, and this park tends to be heavily booked in October. Plan to reserve accommodations here several months in advance if you are a fall foliage fan.

The highlight of the summer is the annual Fourth of July fireworks display over the lake, and attending this takes some planning, too, since it attracts thousands of spectators and there is only one road in and out of the park. Pack a cooler, preferably one with wheels, and bring lawn chairs or a blanket. Arrive just after lunchtime and stake a claim on the grassy hillside

A bull elk at sunrise. Elk Watch trips are conducted from Buckhorn Lake State Resort Park in fall and winter.

overlooking the lake and lodge. Teams of pyrotechnicians launch fireworks from the beach, and these explode over the lake in brilliant red, white, blue, green, and gold displays reflected in the water. The colors are supplemented by the running lights of anchored boats. Each time one of the rockets bursts, the resulting boom rolls around the mountains surrounding the lake, echoing from one to another.

Buckhorn has a good reason for a wintertime visit, too, and one especially appropriate to the park's name. Members of the park's staff lead elk tours to the nearby Robinson Forest, where the animals have been released as part of the state's elk restoration project. Vans leave the lodge before dawn, since the elk are active right after sunrise. They might be far bigger than wildflowers, but the elk are harder to see. Their gray-brown coats blend with the winter landscape. But if you arrive at just the right time, you may be lucky enough to see one of the large bulls, antlers held high, in profile at the top of a treeless ridge.

FACILITY DETAILS

Lodge: Walls of windows in the sandstone Buckhorn Lodge overlook the lake. The spacious lobby has a beautiful, copper-hooded fireplace and lots of comfortable, contemporary sofas and chairs. The park's gift shop is just off the lobby. There are 36 rooms, all with patios and balconies facing the water or the mountains. The restaurant, the Bowlingtown Country Kitchen, seats 220.

Cottages: There are only three cottages, and they cling to a mountainside near the lodge. Two have two bedrooms and one has three bedrooms. These are good choices for a self-catered, extended stay.

Trails: In addition to the Moonshiner's Hollow Trail, there is the 0.5-mile Leatherwood Trail, a loop that takes hikers to a lake overlook. It is relatively short but, like the surrounding mountain roads, seems much longer since it has some very steep grades along the route.

Visitors zip across Buckhorn Lake.

Fishing and Boating: There are many little inlets along the shoreline where you can take your boat and cast for muskie, channel catfish, largemouth and Kentucky bass, crappie, and bluegill. The park marina has lots of free slips for your own boat. It also rents pontoon boats and fishing boats. The lake is popular with jet ski riders.

Swimming: The lodge swimming pool and the lakefront sandy beach are open Memorial Day through Labor Day.

Other Recreation: The 18-hole miniature golf course, laid out within hemlock, ash, and poplar woods, is one of the most scenic in the parks system. The park has a tennis court, shuffleboard court, sandpit volleyball court, and horseshoe pits. A fulltime recreation director oversees a variety of other activities for guests, including children.

EASTERN

Special Events: Fourth of July Fireworks, Fall Elk Watch (September–October), Winter Elk Watch (January–February).

MORE TO EXPLORE

Venture into the town of Buckhorn, about half an hour's drive from the park, to see the Log Cathedral. It is a beautiful, Scandinavian-style church built in 1928. If the door is locked, go to the general store across the street and ask for the key. You can wander around the building as long as you like. Presbyterian services are held on Sundays.

EASTERN

Kentucky Highway 15
Sassafras, KY 41759
(606) 642-4050
http://www.parks.ky.gov/findparks/recparks/cc/
29 acres; 750 lake acres

CARR CREEK STATE PARK is essentially a campground and a beach. The campsites are arranged in a pair of loops ringed by trees, so even though the park is situated on a little peninsula jutting into Carr Creek Lake, you will not see the water from any of the sites. The beach is popular with area residents, who use it frequently during the humid Kentucky summers. Mostly wooded mountains surround the lake. But since the park is located deep in eastern Kentucky coal country, you can see bare patches from strip mining. In fact, a power station built on a former mining site dominates the view from the beach.

EASTERN

The longest sandy beach in the Kentucky state parks system is found at Carr Creek State Park.

On a map, Carr Creek looks pretty close to Buckhorn Lake State Resort Park, which is actually 39 road miles away. This can take you an hour or so to navigate, given the twisting mountain roads. But that park does not have a campground, so if you are camping your way through the region and want to visit Buckhorn, Carr Creek is your best overnight option.

FACILITY DETAILS

Campground: All of the 39 sites have utilities hookups. The large central building with showers, restrooms, and laundry facilities is well maintained. Open from mid-March to mid-November.

Fishing and Boating: A marina, which is not part of the park, is located across Highway 15. You can rent a boat there. Walleye, bass, and crappie are among the fish stocked in the lake. Marshy habitat along some portions of the lakeshore is unusual for this mountainous part of the state, and you may spot herons and ducks more often seen in flatter areas.

Swimming: Carr Creek's is the longest sandy beach in the Kentucky state parks system. Open from Memorial Day to Labor Day.

Other Recreation: There are picnic tables located in the campgrounds.

MORE TO EXPLORE

Carr Creek State Park is about 15 miles south of Hazard. It is worth a side trip to the town to see one of the most unusual buildings anywhere. The Mother Goose House is built of sandstone and topped with a green-shingled roof in the shape of a goose's head and back. The windows are egg shaped. This bit of architectural whimsy was completed in 1940. Since it is a private home, you cannot tour it, but it is a great photo op. For more information, go to http://www.hazardkentucky.com/more/goose.htm.

CARTER CAVES STATE RESORT PARK

344 Caveland Drive
Olive Hill, KY 41164-9032
(606) 286-4411 or (800) 325-0059
http://www.parks.ky.gov/findparks/resortparks/cc/
2,000 acres; 45 lake acres

A T LEAST 20 CAVES pocket the earth beneath Carter Caves State Resort Park, and if you have never been in a cave before, the tours here provide a splendid introduction to the underground world. Guided tours of four caves are offered. Cascade Cave and X Cave are open year-round. Tours of Saltpetre Cave and Bat Cave are added in the summer. Experienced spelunkers can get permits to explore several of the park's other caverns, too.

The tour of Cascade Cave begins with a slightly Gothic touch. Your guide will open a creaking metal door set in the hillside and, with a wave of his flashlight, usher your party into a vast underground room. This is the Dance Hall, where, before it became part of the state park, the previous owner held regular dances. Today, visitors are invited to bring lawn chairs for summer evening movies.

There is plenty of headroom, but the ceiling is low in proportion to the space, and that makes it all the easier to spot some of the cave's inhabitants. The guide keeps an eye out for favorite roosting places, and a flashlight beam, skating across the nooks and crannies in the ceiling, often picks out a sleeping cluster of little bats clinging with their hooked claws to cracks in the stone, snuggled together for warmth. They are probably the common *Myotis lucifugus,* the little brown bat, explains the guide. But they could be *Myotis soda-*

The federally endangered Indiana bat is protected in a Kentucky state nature preserve within Carter Caves State Resort Park.

The Lake Room in Cascade Cave.

lis, the Indiana bat, an endangered species that lives in Carter Caves State Resort Park. Bat Cave is one of a handful of remaining hibernation sites for the species. Thousands of Indiana bats overwinter here. It is the reason for one of two Kentucky state nature preserves within the park's boundaries.

You will continue down a sloping corridor illuminated by banks of electric lights tucked along the edges. The cave is cool, about 50 degrees Fahrenheit, and quiet except for the faint dripping of water that continues to carve out the cavern ever so slowly. The guide will tell you all about the geology, about how water wears away at the limestone, leaving behind various rock formations. Stalactites are the cones "sticking tight" to the ceiling and hanging down. Stalagmites are, therefore, the other ones, the cones seeming to grow up from the floor. Wavy sheets of banded rock have evocative names such as "cave drapery" and "cave bacon."

The corridor leads into another large space. A still, silvery pool reflecting the sky visible through a large opening in the opposite wall dominates

A participant in the January Crawlathon explores the Cathedral Room in Cascade Cave.

the Lake Room. You will walk along a pathway that skirts the sandy shore of the lake and then head out into the open. The forest is just beyond a scattering of boulders, and poking up from the thin soil are several little evergreen shrubs. This plant is the centerpiece of the other state nature preserve within the park. It is the Canadian yew, *Taxus canadensis,* a threatened species that thrives in the habitat protected by the geology of the park.

The tour continues through another cave opening into the Cathedral Room, which takes its name from a rock formation resembling a pipe organ. A rock shelf containing several lumpy stalagmites that look somewhat like misshapen little people dominates one side of the cavern. It is in the Cathedral Room that you will experience that state possible only when you are underground. The guide switches off the lights, and for a few breathless seconds, the cave is enveloped by absolute, total darkness.

You will retrace your steps to leave the cave and follow a short trail to another underground opening. This leads down a narrow passage to the

EASTERN

The large-flowered trillium blooms in April at Carter Caves State Resort Park.

park's underground waterfall. It is an interesting feature, but do not get your hopes up based on the waterfall designation. Since the water gushes 30 feet down a vertical cylinder in the rock, it is more like a giant downspout than a troglodytic Niagara.

As fascinating and beautiful as they are, the caves are not the only attraction at the park. More than 26 miles of hilly, wooded trails loop through Carter Caves State Resort Park. Many of these pass along cliff edges or streambeds. Spring is an especially good time for wildflower enthusiasts to visit; in April and May, 2-mile Horn Hollow Trail has such conspicuous and beautiful flowers as the big white trillium (*Trillium grandiflora*) growing along it.

The time you will not want to visit—unless you are a participant, of course—is during the Crawlathon held every year on the last weekend in January. As the name suggests, some serious wriggling through tight, muddy spaces takes place, and the park is packed with coverall-clad, booted, and helmeted cavers. If you are interested in joining in, check out the details at http://www.crawlathon.com/.

FACILITY DETAILS

Cave Tours: In addition to Cascade Cave, tours are conducted daily in X Cave, which gets its name from the crossing of two passages. Between Memorial Day and Labor Day, you can also tour Bat Cave and Saltpetre Cave. The latter was the site for gunpowder making in the 19th century. If you have caving experience, you can apply for permits to explore other caves in the park.

Lodge: The fieldstone lodge, surrounded by woodlands, has 28 rooms and a 100-seat restaurant. Each room in the lodge has a patio or balcony facing the trees.

Cottages: Eleven two-bedroom cottages with covered decks overlooking the park's hilly landscape are located in the park and have easy access to the trail system. They can sleep up to 10. Nine of the cottages have wood-burning fireplaces.

Campground: The campground has 59 campsites with utilities hookups and 30 tent sites without. There are also two group camp buildings in the primitive campground, each with six bunk beds without mattresses. You will need to bring your own bedding. But with electrical plugs and lights (not to mention solid walls), this can be a good, dry alternative to tent camping. Open mid-March to mid-November.

Swimming: A swimming pool, located 0.5 mile from the lodge, is free to lodge and cottage guests and available to campers and the general public for a small charge.

Gift Shop: The shop is located in the welcome center, where you get tickets for cave tours and permits for your own exploration. You can also pick up a plastic bat or two and videos and books about caves.

Trails: There are 26 miles of trails, including the multi-use, 10-mile Kiser Hollow Trail set up for hikers, mountain bikers, and horseback riders. Guided horse and pony rides are available seasonally. Keep in mind that there is some steep terrain in the park. The Natural Bridge Trail takes you to the park's sandstone arch, which is the only natural bridge in the state that supports a paved highway. There are other arches in the park, too.

Fishing and Boating: The long, narrow Smokey Valley Lake is the state's only trophy bass lake. It also has bluegill, catfish, and crappie. The shape of the lake makes it excellent for canoeing, and guided tours are offered.

EASTERN

Other Recreation: The park has a 9-hole golf course with pro shop, an 18-hole miniature golf course, two tennis courts, and guided nature walks with the park naturalist. Picnic tables, grills, and playgrounds are scattered throughout the park. Two shelters are available for rental.

Special Events: Crawlathon (January), Pioneer Life Week with Revolutionary War and War of 1812 reenactments (July), Mountain Music Gathering (September), Haunted Trail (October).

MORE TO EXPLORE

The utterly charming Kentucky Folk Art Center is located in Morehead, about 40 minutes from the park. Its gift shop is filled with items made by many of the artists whose work is on display here. Go to http://www.morehead-st.edu/kfac/ for a preview.

CUMBERLAND FALLS
STATE RESORT PARK

7351 Kentucky Highway 90
Corbin, KY 40701
(606) 528-4121 or (800) 325-0063
http://www.parks.ky.gov/findparks/resortparks/cf/
1,776 acres

A s is the case with any rushing water, you will hear Cumberland Falls before you see it. But even that preview will not prepare you for the 125-foot-wide wall of water that plunges 68 feet over a sheer drop to the broken boulders at its base, churning up clouds of white and green foam. There is nothing else like it in Kentucky, and for its size and beauty, Cumberland Falls has been called the Niagara of the South.

Canada and New York's larger, more famous falls cannot boast a unique feature of Kentucky's. For a few nights each month, when the moon is full and the sky is clear, you can see a band of light shimmering in the watery mist generated by the falls. This is a moonbow, and it is the only one known to occur on a predictable basis in the Western Hemisphere. (The only other regularly occurring moonbow in the world is at Victoria Falls on Africa's Zambezi River, between Zimbabwe and Zambia.)

Exploring the river just below the falls.

Cumberland Falls, the Niagara of the South, in autumn.

Seeing the moonbow can be a tricky business. In the summer, skies can be overcast. Spring and fall can be rainy. Winter nights are more often clear, but when the temperature drops, the wet rock overlooks to the falls can become hazardously icy, and park officials close them to the public. You may have to visit more than once before you get to see this rare natural phenomenon.

But the falls themselves, with or without the moonbow, are well worth the trip. You can even feel and taste them, not experiences you can say you have had with many other natural wonders. The best way to do this is to take the Moonbow Trail to the lower observation deck, reached by a series of steps. It juts out over the river and puts you level with the center of the giant curtain of water. Spray thrown up from where the water crashes into the rocks of the river will coat your face. Stick your tongue out and you can taste it.

The park contains some lesser falls, too, and hikers will enjoy the challenge of, and the scenery along, the 1.5-mile trail leading to the 44-foot Eagle Falls.

FACILITY DETAILS

Lodge: The charming 51-room Dupont Lodge is perched on a cliff overlooking the Cumberland River. With casement windows, awnings, and tiered flowerbeds, it looks like a European boutique hotel. The original lodge, built by the Civilian Conservation Corps in 1933, burned in 1940. The current one was rebuilt in 1941 in much the same style, with hemlock beams, knotty pine paneling, and large stone fireplaces in the lobby and commons areas. A wide, stone-walled patio is located off the lobby. Both it and the restaurant have views of the river. The lodge rooms were renovated in 2006. The park's Olympic-size pool is a short walk from the lodge.

Cottages: The one- and two-bedroom CCC-built cottages have wonderful touches, such as hand-carved woodwork, inglenooks by the stone fireplaces, and decks overlooking wooded ravines. Two-bedroom cottages have two bathrooms, too. The newer Woodland Rooms are duplexes near the lodge.

Campground: There are 50 wooded campsites with utilities hookups. A 0.5-mile path from the campground leads to the Cumberland River Trail along the water and the Civilian Conservation Corps Memorial Trail, which goes to the lodge. Also, an area for tent camping is located within the Wildflower Loop Trail. Open from mid-March to mid-November.

Visitor Center and Gift Shop: Exhibits explain the geology and history of the park. There are

A resting spot along the Eagle Falls Trail at Cumberland Falls State Resort Park.

EASTERN

Driftwood deposited along a trail near the Cumberland River, just below Cumberland Falls.

many artifacts from the American Indians who lived here for thousands of years. Do take heed of the safety instructions about trails and cliffs that are given here. A gift shop across the sidewalk has books about falls history as well as crafts, candy, and gifts.

Trails: There are about 20 total miles of trails in the park and most of them are hilly, so be aware that your knees will get a workout. The 0.25-mile Laurel Trail, lined with mountain laurel shrubs, is a good route to the falls if you are staying in cabins 501–15. A portion of the 260-mile Sheltowee Trace backcountry trail, which winds through the Daniel Boone National Forest, also passes through the park. Sheltowee ("Big Turtle") was the name the Shawnees gave Boone. A turtle stencil marks the trail.

Fishing and Boating: Bank fishing of the river for bass, catfish, panfish, and roughfish is popular. The park arranges guided rafting trips for guests May through October. Guided canoe trips are conducted by park staff several times of the year. Check with the lodge staff for details.

Other Recreation: Seasonal guided horseback trail rides are offered from the park stables. There are tennis courts, horseshoe pits, and shuffleboard courts next to the lodge. The picnic area with tables, grills, and playgrounds is across the road from the lodge entrance.

Special Events: Backpacking 101 (several times a year), Native American Weekend (March), Overnight Canoe Adventures (April, May, October), Nature Photography Weekend (April), Birding and Wildflower Weekend (May), Kentucky Hills Craft Festival (September), Moonbow Trail Trek (November).

MORE TO EXPLORE

Since the park is surrounded by the Daniel Boone National Forest, there are many wilderness hiking opportunities. The 4,500-acre Beaver Creek Wilderness Area, near Cumberland Falls, is accessed by foot only. Maps and other information are available from the park ranger office at Sterns. Go to http://www.fs.fed.us/r8/boone/districts/stearns/beaver_creek.shtml.

If you have decided to collect waterfalls walks, you can also venture outside the park for a couple of notable big splashes. Yahoo Falls is 113 feet high, nearly twice the height of Cumberland Falls, but it is nowhere near as wide. It is 20 miles' drive from the park, and the hike to it is 0.25 mile. The gruesomely named Dog Slaughter Falls are found near the state park in the Daniel Boone National Forest. Reached by crossing a small footbridge and taking a 2.7-mile trail, these small-scale falls have a beautiful setting, with no suffering canines in sight.

EASTERN

DR. THOMAS WALKER STATE HISTORIC SITE

4929 Kentucky 459
Barbourville, KY 40906
(606) 546-4400
http://www.parks.ky.gov/findparks/histparks/tw/
12 acres

EASTERN

ON ANY WEEKEND in the summer, the grounds at this little park near Barbourville are crowded with families using its picnic tables and shelters. Children race up and down the hillsides, teens pound a ball back and forth on the basketball court, and the smell of grilling meat fills the air.

At the center of this activity, surrounded by tall maple trees and tulip poplars, sits a tiny log cabin. It looks like a child's playhouse, and it is all but ignored by the park visitors. This is a replica of the very first house built in Kentucky by a white person, erected on this spot (or very close by) in 1750. That person was Dr. Thomas Walker, a surveyor and physician who led a six-man expedition sponsored by the Loyal Land Company of Virginia through the Cumberland Gap 17 years ahead of Daniel Boone.

Walker and his party were looking for habitable land that the Virginia firm could market to potential settlers. Instead, they encountered a formidable wilderness. During their 20-week journey, the men were attacked by Shawnees and Cherokees, had to treat their horses for snake bites, and had one of their

Miniature golf is popular at Dr. Thomas Walker State Historic Site.

dogs killed by a bull elk. But they did not go hungry. Walker recorded in his journal,

> We killed 13 buffalos, 8 elks, 53 bears, 20 deer, 4 wild geese, about 150 turkeys, besides small game. We might have killed three times as much meat, if we had wanted it.

Think about how many pounds of meat per man per day this would be! Surely the 13 buffalo alone would have been enough to keep them well fed. But they were on the move, too, and these were obviously pre-cooler days.

The cabin stays locked, but you can look inside through the barred windows. There is a fireplace at one end and a rough-hewn table. Even with a fireplace, this would have been a pretty cold shelter in the winter. No wonder Walker returned to Virginia well before autumn.

A replica of the first log cabin in Kentucky is preserved at Dr. Thomas Walker State Historic Site.

FACILITY DETAILS

Gift Shop: The small gift shop carries a selection of drinks and snacks. Open mid-March to mid-November.

Recreation: There are two rentable picnic shelters, several picnic tables with grills, a nine-hole miniature golf course, playground equipment, a basketball court, and horseshoe pits.

MORE TO EXPLORE

A significant site associated with a pioneer of a very different stripe can be visited in Corbin about a half hour northwest of the Walker cabin. The Colonel Harland Sanders Cafe and Museum sits at the intersection of U.S. Highways 25E and 25W. It is where the colonel cooked up his first batches of Kentucky fried chicken. The recipe was the basis of what would eventually become an international fast-food chain. For details, go to http://www.chickenfestival.com/sanders.htm.

EASTERN

FISHTRAP LAKE STATE PARK

2204 Fishtrap Road
Pikeville, KY 41501
(606) 437-7496
http://www.parks.ky.gov/findparks/recparks/ft/
300 acres; 1,071 lake acres

IT MUST BE FRUSTRATING to be an aspiring Little Leaguer living in the mountains of eastern Kentucky. Where could there possibly be enough flat, open space to build a ball diamond? One unlikely but excellent location turned out to be at the base of Fishtrap Lake Dam. At 195 feet, this is the highest dam in the state, and it would no doubt provide some serious bragging rights if a batter could swat a homer over the top.

The ball field (which even has lights for night games) notwithstanding, most people venture here to fish on the lake, which takes its name from the cage-like wooden devices the pioneers noticed the American Indians using to catch fish. Using more modern technology, the species you are likely to hook include catfish, bluegill, longear sunfish, and hybrid striped, largemouth, and smallmouth bass. The park has a marina and ramps if you want to take a boat out on the lake. Many anglers also seem to find the fishing good in the spillway at the base of the dam.

FACILITY DETAILS

Campground: This is maintained by the Army Corps of Engineers and is located beyond the boat ramp on the western shore of the lake.

Marina: Bait, fuel, and other supplies are available at the marina.

Trail: Eagle Scouts have created a short, self-guided nature trail that begins after you cross a small bridge east of the parking lot.

Other Recreation: A basketball court, playground, and picnic facilities are located in the park. Large picnic shelters overlooking the Levisa Fork of the Big Sandy River are found downstream from the dam and are available for rental. Many picnickers like to decorate the shelters to fit the occasion of a birthday party, holiday, or family reunion.

A birthday party in one of the picnic shelters at Fishtrap Lake State Park.

MORE TO EXPLORE

About a half hour's drive from the park on U.S. Highway 23/119 is one of Kentucky's most significant geological features. The road cut-through at Pound Gap in Pine Mountain exposed a spectacular layering of rock strata dating from the Devonian era, some 400 million years ago. It was the first location in Kentucky to be designated a Distinguished Geologic Site by the Kentucky Society of Professional Geologists. The state highway department has thoughtfully provided a pull-off viewing area on the roadside opposite the towering rock face. You can see a picture at http://www.kspg.org/pages/ipound.html.

GRAYSON LAKE STATE PARK

314 Grayson Lake Park Road
Olive Hill, KY 41164
(606) 474-9727
http://www.parks.ky.gov/findparks/recparks/gl/
1,512 acres; 1,500 lake acres

THE COMBINATION of American beech and eastern hemlock dominating the same mature forest is relatively unusual. For both species to thrive, there has to be the right combination of moisture and sheltered terrain. This happy convergence of ecological circumstances is found at Grayson Lake State Park, and the opportunity to hike the 0.8-mile Beech-Hemlock Trail is an excellent reason in itself to visit the park.

You will find the trailhead behind campsite 28. The contrast between the bright sunshine in the campground and the peaceful gloom of the woods is striking. So is the difference between the smooth, light gray bark of the

The Beech-Hemlock Trail winds through the unusual combination of the two tree species at Grayson Lake State Park.

beeches and the feathery, dark green needles of the hemlocks. Spongy gray-green moss and an abundance of ferns grow here, too. Walk as softy as possible and you may be lucky enough to encounter a white-tailed deer.

The trail is hilly and winds its way toward the lake. When you emerge from the trees, you will be in a little inlet surrounded on three sides by large boulders and opening onto the long lake with sandstone bluffs on the opposite side of the water. Look closely at the boulders and you will see one that has earned the name Lizard Head Rock. It is one of those curious formations that have weathered to resemble nongeological shapes.

The other good way to appreciate the geology of the park is by boat. It is a long, narrow lake and often very quiet once anglers have reached their

Lizard Head Rock is an unusual sandstone formation seen from the Beech-Hemlock Trail.

fishing spots. On a journey west along the lake, the water is dominated on both sides by the sandstone bluffs, which rise as high as 150 feet in places. It is easy to understand why this sheltered, game-rich landscape was a favorite camping area for Cherokees and Shawnees.

Campers play a game of cornhole at Grayson Lake State Park.

FACILITY DETAILS

Campground: Only a few small groups of trees dot the 71-site campground, so most sites are not shaded. This is great if you like to stargaze. But it can get very uncomfortably hot in the summer. Happily, the well-maintained restroom and shower buildings are air-conditioned. Prime sites are at the edge of the woods, numbers 26–29. Open from mid-March to mid-November.

Trails: In addition to the Beech-Hemlock Trail, there is a three-mile loop called the Lick Falls Overlook Trail, which you access from the shorter trail. It offers some challenging hiking and leads to a small waterfall that usually runs only in winter or spring, unless it is an especially wet summer. Part of the trail snakes along cliff tops, providing excellent vistas of the lake's sandstone bluffs. Another portion of the trail follows an old roadbed, and you may very well spy wildlife including turkey and deer. Ruffed grouse are abundant here, too, because they favor beechnuts as food. Allow yourself at least two hours to hike the trail.

Fishing and Boating: A launching ramp off a large parking lot gives lake access to boats. The 74.2 miles of shoreline range from gentle slopes to scenic canyons. A marina renting fishing boats and pontoon boats is three miles from the lake. Call (606) 474-4513. It has a small grocery. You can also purchase bait to use when fishing for bass, bluegill, catfish, crappie, and trout.

Swimming: From the same parking lot that serves the boat ramp, there are steps leading down to the lake's beach, open for swimming from Memorial Day to Labor Day.

EASTERN

Golf Course: The back nine holes of the Hidden Cove Golf Course live up to its name. Tall trees line the fairways. There are occasional views of the lake. Large white sand bunkers provide contrast to the vivid emerald greens. But since several holes of the front nine are near the park's trails and campground, watch for the occasional lost hiker who may inadvertently wander onto the course, not to mention the deer that populate the park. *Golf Digest* rated this the number four Most Affordable New Public Golf Course in the United States in 2005.

Other Recreation: Picnic shelters and tables, playgrounds, horseshoe pits, volleyball and basketball courts.

MORE TO EXPLORE

If you are not a camper but want to stay overnight in the area so you can explore the trails here, two state resort parks are within an hour's drive of Grayson Lake—Carter Caves and Greenbo Lake.

EASTERN

GREENBO LAKE STATE RESORT PARK

965 Lodge Road
Greenup, KY 41144
(606) 473-7324 or (800) 325-0083
http://www.parks.ky.gov/findparks/resortparks/go/
3,008 acres; 225 lake acres

M UCH OF THE DRIVE from I-64 to Greenbo Lake State Resort Park takes you past farms built on the rich bottomland of the Little Sandy River. So the rugged landscape of the park comes as a surprise. The entrance is reached after a long climb up Kentucky 1711. Flat fields have given way to forested hills. The beautiful, still Greenbo Lake, the surface of which reflects the surrounding trees, branches into several of the park's valleys.

Because so many aspects of the park seem intimate—the narrow lake, the cozy 36-room lodge, the one-room schoolhouse near the entrance—Greenbo Lake State Resort Park is the source of a second surprise. It is one of Kentucky's largest state parks. (Only Dale Hollow Lake, Lake Barkley, Lake Cumberland, and Breaks Interstate parks have more land area.) On the more than two dozen miles of trails, you can walk for hours and feel as though you have the woods to yourself. But you probably will not.

This is a popular park, attracting visitors from nearby Ohio and West Virginia, as well as from Kentucky. Named for both

Fishing from the shore of Greenbo Lake.

Facing page:
A stand of
native giant
cane is located
just inside the
entrance to
Greenbo Lake
State Resort
Park.

Greenup County, in which it is located, and neighboring Boyd County, many of the frequent events at the park, such as music and crafts festivals, attract lots of local participants, too.

Many miles of the trails here are demanding. But you do not have to be a die-hard hiker to enjoy a quiet walk. Park in the little lot near the fishing pier and take the path 0.25 mile up and back along the lake. Sycamores and pines dominate here, and a thick layer of pine needles cushions your feet. It is part of the 1-mile Fern Valley Trail, and it provides a fine view of the water and the wooded hillside climbing up from the nearby, opposite, shore.

FACILITY DETAILS

Lodge: The handsome fieldstone Jesse Stuart Lodge is named for the Greenup County native and Kentucky poet laureate, who was born nearby in 1906. You will see display cases featuring a changing exhibit of Stuart's writing memorabilia and first editions just inside the entrance. The lodge, overlooking the lake, has 36 rooms and the Anglers Cove Restaurant. Rocking chairs near the lobby's large stone fireplace are good seats in which to relax to read a book or watch the big-screen television. The gift shop stocks all of Jesse Stuart's in-print books, and there is a small reading room with several of his titles as well. Up a short flight of stairs just off the lobby is a landing with a working model of an iron furnace. Put a quarter in the slot and the whirring, glowing mechanism will spring into action.

Campground: There are 58 sites with utilities hookups and 35 primitive sites situated at the far end of the wooded campground sheltered by hills. In addition to the usual service buildings and a grocery, picnic shelters and playgrounds are placed conveniently around the area. Open from mid-March to mid-November. This is also the site for the annual December display of holiday lights.

Amphitheater: The theater opened in spring 2007 and is the venue for a variety of concerts, plays, and festivals. Patrons need to bring their own lawn chairs or blankets. Check with the park about specific events.

Schoolhouse and Iron Furnace: On your left as you enter the park, you will see a tall, dense stand of native Kentucky cane (a relative of bamboo) and a little white frame schoolhouse. The one-room Clay Lick School operated from 1926 to 1950. Its only heat in winter came from the potbellied stove in the center of the room. As a young man, local author Jesse Stuart

EASTERN

Writing
memorabilia of
Kentucky author
Jesse Stuart
are on display
in the lodge at
Greenbo Lake
State Resort
Park.

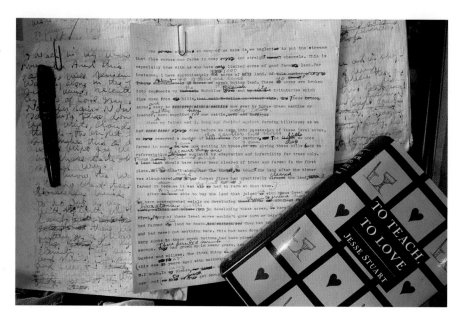

taught in a school not unlike this one. He wrote about his experience in *The Thread That Runs So True*. Across the parking lot from the school are the ruins of Buffalo Iron Furnace, one of several such facilities that used to operate in this area.

Trails: More than 25 miles of multiuse trails loop though the park's wooded, hilly landscape. Hikers, horseback riders, and mountain bikers have access to all or part of each. The shortest walk is the 1-mile Fern Valley Trail. Its route takes you from below the lodge and along the lake. It has interpretive stations about plants and geological features encountered along the way. The other three trails are considerably longer. The Michael Tygart Loop Trail and Claylick Loop Trail are each 7 miles long, and Carpenter's Run Trail is 10 miles. They offer a combination of forest ridge and waterside views.

Fishing and Boating: Greenbo Lake has an interesting wishbone shape. It is long, narrow, and deep. The water is also very clear. Fish obviously thrive in it, since two state records for largemouth bass have been set here. Other stocked species include bluegill, crappie, catfish, and trout. Bank fishing is popular. Or you can choose to fish off the pier on the far side of the community swimming pool. A marina on another arm of the lake is open from April 1 to October 3. Pontoon boats, rowboats, canoes, and motorboats can be rented, but no jet skis are permitted on the lake. One reason this is such a quiet place to fish is that the entire lake is idle only; no wake speeds are allowed.

Swimming: A swimming pool next to the lodge is for use by lodge guests only. A community pool overlooks the tip of the lake near the amphitheater and has a water slide and rain tree for kids. Swimming is not permitted in the lake itself. Pools are open Memorial Day to Labor Day.

Other Recreation: You will find an 18-hole miniature golf course in the camping area. Other facilities are tennis and basketball courts and horse-shoe pits. The park's recreation director plans events year-round for all age groups. There are picnic shelters near the community pool and in the campground.

Special Events: Iron Furnace Road Rally (March), Model Train Railroad Show (March), Quilt Show (April), Dogwood Writers Conference (April), Tri-State Tractor Show (May), Greenbo Lake Jr. Fishing Tournament (July), Colonel Bill Williams Greenup Heritage Music Festival (August), Jesse Stuart Weekend (September), Antique Weekend (November), Holiday Lights (December). Hiking and backpacking events occur throughout the year.

MORE TO EXPLORE

Greenup County has two 19th-century covered bridges, one of which is still open to traffic. The younger of the two, Oldtown, crosses the Little Sandy River. It was built in 1888 and reconstructed in 1999. It is open to foot traffic only. It is on County Road 705, just off Kentucky 1; you may see it on the right if you are going to the park from I-64. Bennett's Mill Bridge crosses Tygart's Creek, just off Kentucky 7, about 8.5 miles south from its junction with U.S. 23. The state historical marker next to the bridge states that it was built about 1855 by brothers B. F. and Pramley Bennett so customers would have access to their mill. For more about the bridges, as well as other area attractions, go to http://www.tourgreenupcounty.com/.

EASTERN

JENNY WILEY STATE RESORT PARK

75 Theatre Court
Prestonsburg, KY 41653
(606) 889-1790 or (800) 325-0142
http://www.parks.ky.gov/findparks/resortparks/jw/
1,498 acres; 1,150 lake acres

As YOU FOLLOW the road leading into the park, you may notice a yellow and brown sign with three human outlines stenciled in black. Two of the figures are tall American Indian warriors. They flank the third, smaller figure of a woman wearing a bonnet, her long skirt almost reaching the ground. She is Virginia Sellards Wiley, whose story is one of the most harrowing in the history of the early American frontier.

On October 1, 1789, a band of American Indians from four tribes attacked the Ballard County, Virginia, log cabin where Jenny lived with her husband Thomas and their four children. Thomas was away, but Jenny's brother was in the home, and he and three of the children were killed. The pregnant Jenny and her infant son were taken captive.

Claimed by a Shawnee chief, she traveled for the next several months throughout eastern Kentucky with her captors. They killed her son because he slowed their progress. When it was born prematurely, the infant she had been carrying met the same gruesome fate.

For nine months, she was forced to work tending camps and planting crops for the American Indians, who tied her up when they went into the forest to hunt. On a rainy summer morning while camped at the falls of Little Mud Creek in what is now Johnson County, the American Indians set off on another hunt. Jenny purposely got her rawhide bonds soaked in the rain, allowing her to pry them loose and escape. She fled to nearby Harman's Station, where a party of long hunters protected her and escorted her back to Virginia.

Jenny and Thomas Wiley had five more children. They eventually settled in Johnson County, Kentucky, where Jenny died and was buried in 1831 at age 71.

A portion of the Jenny Wiley Trail, which stretches north through the mountains from the park named in her memory to Greenbo Lake State Resort Park, can be followed here. If you are a driver, not a hiker, the Jenny Wiley Scenic Byway loops along eastern Kentucky roads. The staff at the lodge desk can give you a map.

Sunset over the marina at Jenny Wiley State Resort Park.

Despite the ordeal of its namesake, this is a notably lovely, peaceful park. The beautiful Dewey Lake is favored by flocks of shorebirds, including many species of ducks, geese, and herons. Mist rises from the trees of the mountains most mornings, blanketing the park grounds and adding to a sense of stillness and isolation.

By the time the mist burns off in late morning, the activity level picks up. The park has a busy disc golf course. Boaters and anglers are out on the lake. During the summer theater season, the park is crowded with visitors who come for the evening performances by Kentucky's only professional acting company east of I-75.

The wading pool near the May Lodge.

FACILITY DETAILS

Lodge: Balconies from the 49 rooms of the May Lodge overlook the swimming pool and the wooded mountains of the park. Since Jenny Wiley State Resort Park is located near U.S. 23, the Country Music Highway, the lodge restaurant is called the Music Highway Grill. No bland Muzak is piped in here. It is all country, all the time. The gift shop off the lobby has a good selection of books by Kentucky authors, as well as craft and food items.

Cottages: Duplex cottages are located near the disc golf course. One- and two-bedroom cottages are set in the woods by the lake. Park trails run near all for easy walking access.

Campground: Three spokes of the 117-site campground branch off from the central service area. On a busy weekend, this feels more like a small city than a campground. On Friday and Saturday nights, line dancing on the concrete dance pad is a very popular activity with campers and area resi-

Plays and musicals are produced during the summer in the amphitheater at Jenny Wiley State Resort Park.

dents. Twenty-eight sites at the tip of the longest spoke are for tent camping. Open from mid-March to mid-November.

Amphitheater: A professional theater company stages plays (mostly musicals) in the 580-seat Jenny Wiley Theatre from mid-June to mid-August. Recent productions have included *Forever Plaid, West Side Story, The Wizard of Oz, A Chorus Line,* and *Disney's High School Musical.* Performances begin at 8:15 p.m. For information about shows and to book tickets, call (606) 886-9274 or (877) 225-5598. Current and upcoming season information can also be found at http://www.jwtheatre.com/.

Trails: A pleasant way to reach the amphitheater from the lodge is to take the Moss Ridge Hiking Trail, which winds through the woods. If you are particularly interested in the flora of the mountains, walk the 0.75-mile Sassafras Trail, whose native plants, such as ground cedar, Christmas fern, and sassafras, are discussed in a brochure you can pick up at the trailhead. The Jenny Wiley Trail (4.5 miles) is the most challenging and begins near cottage 132.

Fishing and Boating: Dewey Lake fish include largemouth and hybrid striped bass, bluegill, catfish, and crappie. Several boat ramps in the park serve the lake. The boat dock has 199 slips and rents pontoon boats.

Jenny Wiley State Resort Park has an 18-hole disc golf course.

Disc Golf Course: The challenging 18-hole disc golf course is laid out in scenic valleys of the park. Many throws are uphill and around trees. You can purchase or rent discs at the course. For more details about the game, go to the Jenny Wiley Disc Golf Club Web site, http://jwdiscgolf.checkoutmypage.com/.

Other Recreation: Picnic tables, grills, and playgrounds are located throughout the park, and picnic shelters are located at the campground. The Stonecrest Golf Course is located next to the park. Its phone number is (606) 886-1006.

Special Events: Elk Viewing Tours (January–March, September– December), Buffalo Night (January, October), Elk Night (October).

MORE TO EXPLORE

Two attractions near the park in Prestonsburg provide very different activities. The Mountain Arts Center (http://www.macarts.com/) is the home of the Kentucky Opry, featuring bluegrass, country, and gospel music concerts. The center also stages exhibits of regional arts and crafts. The East Kentucky Science Center (http://www.wedoscience.org/) has a planetarium and regularly changing traveling science exhibits.

EASTERN

KINGDOM COME STATE PARK

502 Park Road
Cumberland, KY 40823
(606) 589-2479
http://www.parks.ky.gov/findparks/recparks/kc/
1,283 acres; 3.5 lake acres

THE NOTABLE STATISTIC about Kingdom Come, situated along the crest of Pine Mountain, is that it is at the highest elevation of any of Kentucky's state parks. You will appreciate this as your car grinds up the 1.5-mile road into the park from Kentucky 119. As the engine whines, the story of the little engine that could may very well come to mind.

The park gets its name from another story. *The Little Shepherd of Kingdom Come* by Kentuckian John Fox Jr. was published in 1903. About a young orphan from the Cumberland Mountains named Chad who got caught up in the chaos of the Civil War, it was America's first million-copy best seller.

One can assume the mountainous landscape here has changed little since Chad's day. The slopes are covered in dense rhododendron thickets, making the park one of the prime habitats in eastern Kentucky for the American black bear. Adults can be 4 to 6.5 feet long and weigh up to 500 pounds. The impressive animals were virtually gone from the state by the middle of the 19th century. But a few years ago, they started moving back into Kentucky from Virginia, Tennessee, and North Carolina and currently have been seen in more than 20 counties. Researchers from the University of

Mountain laurel blooms along the Raven Rock Trail at Kingdom Come State Park.

EASTERN

A wildlife biologist keeps four black bear cubs warm while his colleagues attach a transmitter to their sedated mother at Kingdom Come State Park. © *The Courier-Journal.*

Kentucky tag and electronically track the bears, so their movements in the park are closely monitored.

You will see signs along roads and trails here (as well as in other eastern Kentucky parks) giving safety advice. "Do not feed the bears" is only part of it. It is a good idea to take a whistle or other noisemaker with you when you hike the trails to scare away curious bruins. Do not try to outrun one. They may look ungainly, but black bears can run 30 miles per hour.

All that said, I did not see a bear during the time I spent on the trails here.

But I did see some breathtaking vistas of the mountains. Using the trails map, I hiked along a cliff edge over bare rock one evening to Log Rock, the park's natural sandstone arch. Although I appreciated the view of the mountains stretching, seemingly endlessly, into Virginia, I was a little chagrined to discover when I got to Log Rock that one of the paved park roads comes right to it.

The other famous geological feature of Kingdom Come is Raven Rock. Located more or less at the geographic center of the park, it cannot be reached by any paved shortcut. The only way to see the 290-foot monolith that leans into the sky at a 45 degree angle is to hike up the very steep Raven Rock Trail.

If your knees survive the trek to the top of Raven Rock Trail and you are keen on even more serious hiking, you should know about Kentucky's newest state park, which is under development and partially open. Pine Mountain Trail State Park encompasses about 1,000 acres in a band along both sides of a 120-mile trail connecting Breaks Interstate Park and Cumberland Gap National Historical Park. About half of the trail is currently open, a portion that runs from Elkhorn City to Kingdom Come State Park. Three overnight shelters are available. Eventually, the mountain ridge trail, designed for hiking and backpacking, will also pass through Bad Branch and Blanton Forest state nature preserves. Go to http://www.pinemountaintrail.com for more information.

FACILITY DETAILS

Bed and Breakfast: Not actually within the park, the Benham School House Bed and Breakfast is located at 100 Central Avenue in Benham, about 20 minutes from the Kingdom Come State Park entrance. It was built in 1926 as the school for children of the Wisconsin Steel Corporation's employees. Former classrooms have been converted to 30 guest rooms. The wide hallways are still lined with lockers. Call (606) 848-3000 for reservations.

Campground: There are 10 sites with utilities hookups located on the grounds of the bed and breakfast. Primitive camping is allowed in the park in designated areas. Check with the park office.

Trails: The Little Shepherd Trail is a narrow gravel and blacktop road that snakes along the crest of Pine Mountain for 38 miles between Whitesburg and Harlan. The overlooks, especially in fall when the trees are in full color,

Sunset over the mountains from the Bullock Overlook.

are marvelous. But there is very little room at many points for two vehicles to pass if they meet. Go slowly. The park has 14 hiking trails, varying in length from 0.1 to 0.8 mile each and covering a total of 5 miles. Many have very steep inclines. If your knees and lungs are up to the stress, many views from the trails across the mountaintops are spectacular.

Fishing and Boating: You can fish from the bank of the 3.5-acre lake for bluegill, largemouth bass, crappie, catfish, and trout. Pedal boats can be rented from April through October.

Cave Amphitheater: A shallow sandstone cave open on one side is furnished with bleachers and is available for meetings. It is reached via a trail from the lake's parking lot.

Other Recreation: Nine-hole miniature golf course, volleyball and basketball courts, picnic shelters and tables, and playgrounds. Open from April through October.

Special Events: Kentucky Black Bear Festival (May).

MORE TO EXPLORE

The Kentucky Coal Mining Museum is across the street from the Benham School House Bed and Breakfast. The three-story building was the Wisconsin Steel commissary. Displays include historical mining equipment, photographs of early-20th-century miners, re-creations of rooms from other buildings in the company town, a model mine, and an exhibit about country music singer Loretta Lynn, the Coal Miner's Daughter. Find more details at http://kentucky.coal.museum/.

LEVI JACKSON WILDERNESS ROAD STATE PARK

998 Levi Jackson Mill Road
London, KY 40744
(606) 330-2130
http://www.parks.ky.gov/findparks/recparks/lj/
896 acres

MILLSTONES BELONG to that rare class of objects that are both extremely utilitarian and curiously artful. One of the attractions at this park is an outdoor display of millstones lining the walkways near McHargue's Mill. Inspection of the collection, the largest in the country, reveals that the pioneers went to the trouble to import heavy stones from Europe. Apparently, Kentucky's soft limestone just could not hold up under repeated grinding, or at least had to be replaced regularly. The carved grinding surfaces result in an interesting variety of patterns.

The log replica working mill, built on the same Little Laurel River site as an earlier one, dominates one end of the mill pond and is the first building you notice when you enter the park from U.S. 25. It is one of many structures that give visitors an idea of what life was like for the early settlers.

A kitchen corner in the Mountain Life Museum.

A collection of millstones lines the path to McHargue's Mill on the banks of the Laurel River.

Farther into the heavily wooded park, you will find the Mountain Life Museum. This is a collection of seven log structures, some moved from other sites and some replicas, that include a school, loom house, church, smokehouse, and barn. All are furnished with period pieces and implements.

The outdoor museum is here because the land the park encompasses contains a significant pioneer intersection. Both the Wilderness Road and Boone's Trace cross it. These were routes used by 18th- and 19th-century settlers traveling westward into Kentucky.

Situated between the mill and the museum is the Defeated Camp Cemetery, a reminder that undertaking the settlement of Kentucky could be a dangerous enterprise. On October 3, 1786, a party of about 60 pioneers was camped on a hilltop near Boone's Trace. It was a moonlit night, and apparently the party decided to party, staying up to dance, sing, and generally let their hair down. Unfortunately, the group had chosen a site sacred to the local Shawnees and Chickamaugas, who, upon discovering the revelers apparently in the act of defiling their sacred place, killed and scalped at least two dozen of them. Their remains are buried here.

You can now safely hike along the wooded remainder of Boone's Trace, which Daniel Boone blazed from the Cumberland Gap to the Kentucky River in 1775. The Wilderness Road, constructed in 1795, is still used as a road. Much of the route it followed was paved in the 20th century and today is Kentucky 223. It runs through the center of the park.

So who was Levi Jackson? He was the first county judge of Laurel County. The land that is now the park was part of the land grant given to his father-in-law, John Freeman, for service in the Revolutionary War. Both Jackson and Freeman family cemeteries can be reached by walking along a path parallel to Kentucky 223.

Redbuds bloom at Mountain Life Museum at Levi Jackson Wilderness Road State Park.

FACILITY DETAILS

Campground: The large, wooded campground has 136 sites, all with utilities hookups. It is supported by a grocery store and three central service buildings with activities room, showers, restrooms, and laundry facilities. There is also a group camping area with special rates. Open year-round.

Museum: The Mountain Life Museum is open from April 1 to October 31. There is an admission fee. The park gift shop is located at the entrance.

Trails: Portions of the Wilderness Road and Boone's Trace make up 8.5 miles of two looping hiking trails.

Swimming: The park has a community swimming pool open daily from Memorial Day to mid-August and on weekends through Labor Day.

Other Recreation: Eighteen-hole miniature golf course, horseshoe pits, and volleyball and basketball courts. Picnic tables, grills, and playgrounds are located throughout the park. There are also four picnic shelters.

Special Events: Laurel County Homecoming (August).

MORE TO EXPLORE

The blacksmith shop in the Mountain Life Museum has bars on the windows, but not because it contains anything of special value that needs protecting. In 1955, some of *The Kentuckian,* starring Burt Lancaster in the title role, was filmed on location here. The little log building was used as a jail in one scene. The movie marked the film debut of Walter Matthau, who played the bad guy.

NATURAL BRIDGE
STATE RESORT PARK

2135 Natural Bridge Road
Slade, KY 40376
(606) 663-2214 or (800) 325-1710
http://www.parks.ky.gov/findparks/resortparks/nb/
2,250 acres; 60 lake acres

SPRING IS A FINE SEASON to visit Natural Bridge State Resort Park, located near Red River Gorge Geological Area on the edge of the vast Daniel Boone National Forest. That is when more than 100 species of wildflowers, delicate pink and yellow lady's slippers among them, bloom in the woods. In summer, flocks of goldfinches and other songbirds cover the hanging birdfeeders on the porch just outside the lodge restaurant. The park's sky lift is predictably popular in the autumn, when the cable ride whisks visitors up a steep mountainside for panoramic views of fall foliage.

But winter may be the best time of all to visit Natural Bridge State Resort Park. With the leaves off the trees, the rocky skeleton of the landscape is laid bare, and the dramatic sandstone arches, including the one that gives the park its name, are fully in view.

By far the busiest trail is the 0.75-mile Original Trail that

Pink lady's slipper blooms in May at Natural Bridge State Resort Park.

The sandstone formation from which the park takes its name.

climbs from its beginning behind the park lodge to Natural Bridge, which, at 65 feet high and 75 feet long, is the largest of 180 natural arches found within a 5-mile radius of the park.

To walk to the arch in winter, clip Yaktrax to your hiking boots, since the rocky slope can be slick with ice. The path ascends through stands of deep green hemlock. The ground is covered with ferns, 45 species of which grow in the park. Icicles hang from the rocky cliff faces. Without birdsong on a frigid January day, the only sound in the forest is of water splashing over the rocks in the stream near the trail. The combination of dense forest and steep mountainsides feels Alpine, and you will half expect to see a Brothers Grimm gnome peering at you out of the gloom.

But you do not have to imagine any forest dwellers. The park is home to scores of bird, reptile, and mammal species, many of which are rare. The habitat here is so varied and so important that almost 1,200 acres within Natural Bridge State Resort Park have been set aside as a Kentucky state nature preserve. One animal it protects is the Virginia big-eared bat (*Corynorhinus townsendii virginianus*), a federally endangered species, which favors the limestone caves in the park. It is a fantastical-looking creature, with pointed ears almost half as long as its body.

If the trip up the mountain and the view from Natural Bridge whet your walking appetite, there are 20 more miles of trails to explore, ranging from 0.25 mile (Lakeside Trail) to 7.5 miles (Sand Gap Trail). Be prepared for some rugged terrain and steep climbs.

Thanks to the popularity of Natural Bridge as a tourist attraction, this was one of Kentucky's original state parks. In the late 19th century, the Kentucky Union Railway built a track through the area to ship timber. Company officials realized that money was also to be made from visitors eager to see the dramatic landscape, so trails and campgrounds were developed. In the early 20th century, the Louisville and Nashville Railroad bought the property and, in 1926, donated it to the state. The first Hemlock Lodge (replaced in 1962 by the current building) opened in 1927.

FACILITY DETAILS

Lodge: Hemlock Lodge has 35 rooms, all with balconies from which you can savor the scenery. The Sandstone Arches Restaurant in the lodge seats 175. A gift shop and meeting rooms are located off the lobby, which is not as spacious or comfortable as those at some other parks, but you will not be lingering here anyway. You will be hiking.

Cottages: Located on the other side of the little lake below the lodge, four of the cottages have two bedrooms and seven have one bedroom. They all have wood-burning fireplaces. There is a boardwalk from the cottage area to several trailheads and to the lodge. Along the way you will find the nature and activities center. Among the center exhibits are displays explaining the geology of the area and the formation of the arches.

Campground: Two campgrounds, Whittleton and Middle Fork, have 82 sites with utilities hookups. There are also 12 primitive sites for tent campers. The Middle Fork Campground is located near Mill Creek Lake. Open from mid-March to mid-November.

Trails: A dozen trails wind through the mountains and valleys of the park. A map with detailed descriptions of each is available at the lodge desk. The geological features Balanced Rock, Battleship Rock, and Henson's Arch are found on trails with those names. Other trails, including Rock Garden, are especially good for wildflowers. Traces of the Mountain Central Railway can be seen along Whittleton Trail. Do not be lulled into overconfidence by the seemingly short lengths of many park trails. A 0.25-mile upward climb seems considerably longer than a flat walk of the same distance. Be very careful along cliff edges, too.

Nightly dances are a popular activity from spring through fall on Hoedown Island at Natural Bridge State Resort Park.

Dancing: A causeway provides access to the one-acre Hoedown Island in the center of the small lake below the lodge. Line dancing, square dancing, and clogging take place on an open-air dance patio on weekend evenings during good weather.

Fishing and Boating: The 54-acre Mill Creek Lake features fishing for bass, bream, catfish, crappie, and rainbow trout. On the Hoedown Island Lake, you can rent pedal boats and hydro-bikes Memorial Day through Labor Day.

Swimming: A pool complex is located between the lake and the cliff beneath Hemlock Lodge. It has a stone bathhouse, an 80,000-gallon zero-depth pool that can be entered without using steps, and a wading pool. The main swimming pool features directional water jets and floor bubblers. Open daily Memorial Day weekend through mid-August and weekends through Labor Day.

Sky Lift: Open daily the first weekend of April through the last weekend in October, the sky lift provides a leisurely ride in ski lift–style chairs to the Natural Bridge arch. If you are scared of heights, hike to the formation instead. The view from the lift is breathtaking but head-spinning.

Other Recreation: The park has an 18-hole miniature golf course, open April 1 to October 31, two snack bars, and four picnic shelters. The picnic area below the cottages has tables along Red River where mature sycamores and other hardwoods line the riverbank and provide shade.

Special Events: Appalachian Heritage Buffalo Night (January), Leave No Trace Beginner Backpacking Workshops (March, September), Wildflower Weekend (April), Herpetology Weekend (May), Winter Bird Weekend (December), Explore Arch Country Guided Hikes (throughout the year).

MORE TO EXPLORE

Once you have worn out your hiking boots, you can enjoy more of the remarkable scenery of the region by driving the 45-mile Red River Gorge National Scenic Byway, which starts along Kentucky 213 and loops back to Natural Bridge on Kentucky 11. For route details, go to http://www.byways.org/explore/byways/2482/.

Also, the Kentucky Reptile Zoo, one of the state's most unusual attractions, is just a few minutes from the park. Hundreds of snakes and several other reptiles are on display here. Venom is extracted from poisonous species, including rattlesnakes, cobras, and mambas, for antivenin and medical research. If you arrive at the right time, you can see the venom extraction taking place behind thick glass. The zoo's Web site is http://www.kyreptilezoo.org/.

EASTERN

PAINTSVILLE LAKE STATE PARK

1151 Kentucky Route 2275
Staffordsville, KY 41256
(606) 297-8486
http://www.parks.ky.gov/findparks/recparks/pl/
242 acres; 1,139 lake acres

EASTERN

A s is the case with many Kentucky state parks, Paintsville Lake State Park is located on the shores of water impounded by a U.S. Army Corps of Engineer dam. Usually, the Army Corps office and the park facilities are well separated. But here, they are within sight of one another, and that can work to a visitor's advantage.

Along Kentucky 2275, which ends at the park entrance, you will see the signs marking the Army Corps office. Take the road, which leads to the top of a hill, and park. The office includes a visitor and information center.

On the other side of the building, you will find benches and a view out over the lake. The park and its marina are spread out below, giving a perspective you do not usually get without a map. While enjoying the view near sunrise or sunset, you may be joined by deer emerging from the surrounding woods to graze on the Army Corps' trim lawn (and flowerbeds).

The park is relatively new, having opened in 1984, and it is as clean and neat as the neighboring military facility.

Broad sidewalks follow the shoreline. There are many benches where you can sit and watch the boats on the lake. If you are traveling with small children, modern playground equipment is also placed lakeside, enabling you to keep an eye on your young Tarzan or Xena and still enjoy the lake view.

This is a popular park with anglers and boaters and something of an insiders' secret with campers. The campground, set back in the woods a little away from the lake, is especially quiet, and chances of seeing wildlife are excellent.

There are no developed trails in the park proper. However, if you want to stretch your legs in the woods instead of along the lake, the local Kiwanis Club maintains a hiking trail off the road leading to the Army Corps office.

FACILITY DETAILS

Campground: The 32 sites with utilities hookups are arranged in a straight line near the lake. Two RV sites with good views of the water are ADA compliant. Ten walk-in tent camping sites (no hookups) are at the very end of

A deer grazes at sunrise near the ranger station overlooking the marina at Paintsville Lake State Park.

Morning coffee at a Rocky Knob Recreation Area campsite at Paintsville Lake State Park.

EASTERN

the campground, nestled in the woods. Service buildings are across from the main entrance to the campground. There is a playground by the parking lot for the tent campers. Open year-round.

Fishing and Boating: Fish include a variety of bass species, redbreast sunfish, and walleye. The marina has 84 open slips, 80 covered slips, and a launching ramp, and it rents fishing boats, houseboats, pedal boats, and pontoon boats. Several other launch ramps are positioned around the lake.

Other Recreation: There are four picnic shelters in the park. The campground also has horseshoe pits, a sand volleyball court, and a basketball court.

Special Events: Bird Migration Walk (first Saturday in May), Creative Arts and Homegrown Music Festival (second weekend in May), Monarch Migration Tag (second and third Saturdays in September), Adult Artists Workshops (several times a year).

MORE TO EXPLORE

On the left side of the road as you enter the park, you will see a collection of log buildings enclosed by a split-rail fence. This is the Mountain Homeplace, a working 19th-century farm demonstrating what the settlements in this part of Appalachia were like more than 150 years ago. In addition to a barn and pasture area with animals such as oxen, horses, and the unusual haired sheep (which have fur rather than wool), there are a school, a church, a farmhouse, and vegetable gardens. The Web site is http://www.mountainhomeplace.com/.

The Mountain Homeplace, a reconstructed pioneer community near Paintsville Lake State Park.

For a glimpse into another aspect of mountain life, venture to Van Lear, about 10 miles away on the other side of Paintsville. At Webb's Grocery, you can get information about Loretta Lynn and Crystal Gayle, the country music stars—and sisters of the store's proprietor—who were born in Butcher Hollow, a collection of ramshackle houses clinging to the slopes in the narrow valley near Van Lear, a town built by a coal mining company. The store stocks souvenirs and recordings of the singers. Tours of Butcher Hollow are run from Webb's. Detailed driving directions are available at the Army Corps visitor center at the lake.

PINE MOUNTAIN STATE RESORT PARK

1050 State Park Road
Pineville, KY 40977
(606) 337-3066 or (800) 325-1712
http://www.parks.ky.gov/findparks/resortparks/pm/
1,519 acres

PINE MOUNTAIN STATE RESORT PARK opened in 1924 as the system's first state park. Trails, shelters, and accommodations were constructed by the Civilian Conservation Corps, and many of these structures still serve the park, which combines a stunning natural setting with many annual traditions that have developed through its decades of operation.

Certainly the foremost of these is the Mountain Laurel Festival, held every May at the height of the flowering shrubs' blooming season. Mountain laurel (*Kalmia latifolia*) is evergreen and so provides color against the rocky outcroppings of the mountains year-round. In May, June, and July, it blooms with clusters of oddly geometric little pink and white flowers, shaped like squat Japanese lanterns when closed and resembling tiny inverted umbrellas when open.

Carnival rides and food, concerts, a golf tournament, and a parade are among the attractions in Pineville and the park. The climax of the festival comes with the crowning of the queen of the Mountain Laurel Festival, chosen from young women from colleges around the state who have been selected as festival princesses. The ceremony, on Saturday afternoon, takes place in the Laurel Cove Amphitheater, ringed by blooming shrubbery. Even more mountain laurel is carried in the

The queen of the Mountain Laurel Festival is given an elaborate laurel bouquet.

bouquets of the white-gowned princesses. Kentucky's sitting governor gives a little speech.

The park's most famous attraction is Chained Rock, an unabashed effort on the part of Pineville's city fathers to create a little tourist buzz. In 1933, local citizens who had formed the Pineville Chained Rock Club, a bunch of Boy Scouts and some strong backs from the CCC (plus a team of mules), hauled a 101-foot-long chain consisting of seven-pound links and attached it to a boulder that appears to be looming over the town below. The chain is anchored to the mountainside allegedly to restrain the rock and keep it from breaking off, rolling downhill, and smashing through Pineville.

If you stand in the parking lot at the grocery in the center of town and look up the mountain, you can just make out the line of the chain, which looks as delicate as a child's gold necklace.

The reason you should hike the mountainous trail with its multiple wooden stairways to Chained Rock is that the view is terrific. Go at dawn, just as the sun is starting to light the surrounding mountain ridges. You will see Pineville and U.S. 25E (part of the original Wilderness Road) in the valley far below. As the temperature warms, the mist from the mountain forests starts to roll into the valley, filling it so that all signs of human occupation are covered in cottony fog. You are alone at the top of the mountain. Maybe.

Take a whistle with you. You will have noticed on your winding drive up to the Chained Rock trailhead that the garbage cans at picnic areas were either heavily reinforced or tipped over, their contents scattered along the ground. This was not the work of vandals. The park is home to a growing population of *Ursus americana*, American black bears.

Slowly driving down the Chained Rock road the evening before my hike, I came around a bend and slammed on my brakes. A young male bear was sitting in the center of the road. He leapt up, ran up the hillside by the road, and hid in a thicket of rhododendron. Obviously as fascinated by my car as I was by him, he poked his head up over the bushes to take another look in my direction, round black ears and pointed snout clearly visible. He was beautiful and adorable—in a large, dangerous animal sort of way. I felt tremendously privileged to have made his acquaintance and tremendously relieved to have done so from within the steel body of my car.

Facing page: Mountain laurel growing in Pine Mountain State Resort Park blooms on Chained Rock as the morning mist rolls into the valley below.

FACILITY DETAILS

Lodge: The stone and wood Herndon J. Evans Lodge, named in honor of a former editor of the *Lexington Herald-Leader,* has 30 rooms, a pair of intimate lobbies featuring large, wood-burning stone fireplaces, and several little patios and balconies that offer fine mountain vistas. The oldest section of the lodge, which was the original park office, is made of sandstone and logs of the now virtually extinct American chestnut. You will notice wildlife prints on the walls of the 125-seat restaurant. They are by noted wildlife artist Ray Harm, who lived in the Pine Mountain area in the 1960s and 1970s. The artworks are just part of the 180-print collection that is on display throughout the lodge complex. The lodge also has an ADA-compliant swimming pool that is open Memorial Day to Labor Day.

Cottages: The 9 one-bedroom log cabins with stone fireplaces and private decks were the original overnight accommodations when the park opened in the 1920s. There are also 11, more modern, two-bedroom cottages.

Trails: The interconnecting network of 14 park trails can get a little confusing. (Yes, that means I got lost on one of my hikes.) The Chained Rock Trail is the best known and most popular, but if you are a plant lover, you should not miss the Fern Garden Trail. It winds through a deep ravine in which towering hemlocks and tulip poplars grow and rhododendron thickets are dense. About halfway along the trail, you will come to a lush carpet of royal and cinnamon ferns. The latter of these can grow up to four feet high during a wet summer. Features of the park's many other trails include footbridges, stairs and shelters built in the 1930s by CCC craftsmen, and natural attractions that include waterfalls, mountain streams, natural arches, and rock shelters.

Nature Center: Located in the lodge complex. The park's naturalist offers programs about area natural and cultural history all year.

Golf Course: The name of the championship 18-hole Wasioto Winds Golf Course means "valley of the deer." But those are not the only animals you may see during a round. Black bears have been known to wander onto the course around dusk, especially around the 17th hole. So do not schedule your tee time too late. Laid out in a valley between two mountains, the course features a practice range, two practice putting greens, and an indoor training center. You can reach the pro shop at (606) 337-1066 or (800) 814-8002.

Other Recreation: The miniature golf course is open April 1 through October 31. Picnic tables, shelters, grills, and restrooms are located near Laurel Cove. Playgrounds are located throughout the park.

Special Events: Elk Viewing Tours (January, September–December), Kentucky Writers Workshop (March), Kentucky Mountain Laurel Festival (May), Great American Dulcimer Convention (September).

MORE TO EXPLORE

The Cumberland Gap National Historical Park is less than 15 miles from Pine Mountain. A visitor center has exhibits about the history and wildlife of the area. You can also see three states (Kentucky, Virginia, and Tennessee) from Pinnacle Overlook, reached via the Skyland Road. The striking bowl-shaped depression in which the town of Middlesboro, Kentucky, is built is noticeable from the overlook. Many geologists think the formation is a meteor crater. For Cumberland Gap National Historical Park information, go to http://www.nps.gov/cuga/.

EASTERN

YATESVILLE LAKE STATE PARK

26762 Kentucky Highway 1185
Louisa, KY 41230
(606) 673-1492
http://www.parks.ky.gov/findparks/recparks/yl/
808 acres; 2,300 lake acres

I**F YOUR IDEA** of the perfect getaway is pottering around the inlets and coves of a lake and sleeping in a tent in the woods, Yatesville Lake State Park will be your ideal. The largest lake in eastern Kentucky, Yatesville Lake has an irregular shape thanks to lots of branches. These just beg to be explored. Take your boat into one for quiet fishing or just a bit of privacy while you are out on the water. When you are ready to call it a day, the park has 16 camping sites accessed from the water. Tie up to the shore and pitch your tent. Camping on a wooded hillside, you get the benefit of both the sounds of the forest and the lapping of water against the shore to soothe you to sleep.

The lake's scenic mountain setting makes it worth a visit even if you do not go out on the water or sleep in the woods. Like all the other lakes in the parks system, this one was built and is maintained by the U.S. Army Corps of Engineers. A popular exercise site for area residents is the paved road that

EASTERN

One of the campsites reached by boat.

EASTERN

gently circles up a mountainside to an observation area near the dam's operating tower.

Since there is a parking area up here, too, you do not have to make the hike, but you will want to stop by near sunset and watch the variety of pleasure craft heading back to the marina in the fading light. The island in the middle of the lake and the various inlets make it seem as though the craft are negotiating a maze, and the elevated view across the water is gorgeous.

No doubt anticipating the vantage point's popularity, the Army Corps thoughtfully placed several benches where you can sit and take in the view until the light fades. Do bear in mind that a gate at the road entrance closes at sunset.

FACILITY DETAILS

Campground: In addition to the 16 boat camping sites, there are 27 sites with utilities hookups, 20 primitive sites, and 4 sites set in the woods, which can be reached by hiking from the main campground. The main campground has a service building and playground. Restrooms are set along a service road behind the boat camping sites. Open from mid-March to mid-November.

Trails: The Mary Ingles Trail System is a series of six trail loops ranging from rugged to ADA compliant. There is also a system of wooded trails (Pleasant Ridge Trail System) and the Yatesville Lake Multiuse Trail, which is more than 20 miles long and open to hikers, mountain bikers, and horseback riders. The short 19th Hole Trail runs just off the golf course.

Fishing and Boating: Of course, you can take a boat onto the lake. Also, just inside the park entrance, there is a lagoon for bank fishing. An ADA-compliant fishing jetty is across the road from the lagoon, and an ADA-compliant trail leads from it along the lakeshore. Bass, bluegill, and crappie are the dominant fish. The marina has 140 boat slips. Pontoon and johnboats can be rented. The marina store has gasoline, groceries, live bait, and fishing tackle. Boat launch ramps can be found at the marina and at the campground.

Golf Course: Thanks to the mountain setting, the elevation changes dramatically as you play the 18-hole, par 71 Eagle Ridge Golf Course. This makes it both challenging and scenic. On some holes you seem to be playing right into the mountains. Deer and wild turkey frequently wander

A view from the dam's observation deck at Yatesville Lake State Park.

across the course. In 2005 *Golf Digest* named this the number three Most Affordable New Public Golf Course in the United States. The fairways were completely renovated in 2007.

Swimming: A public beach area near the marina has playgrounds, restrooms, and showers.

MORE TO EXPLORE

At the Louisa exit from U.S. 23, the one to take to get to the park, you will see a large pavilion topped with a blue-tiled, peaked roof. The Exxon Marketplace is part gas station, part convenience store, part fast-food stop, and part cultural museum. Because so many stars were born in the towns along its route, U.S. 23 is known as the Country Music Highway. Large markers along the route tell who was born where. The owner of the Exxon Marketplace, a country music fan, displays many items in his collection of memorabilia here. Signed guitars and clothing (boots, jackets, and dresses) of the Judds, Hylo Brown, Ricky Skaggs, Tammy Wynette, George Jones, and others are mounted high on the wall above refrigerated drinks cases. But the high point of the collection may be Elvis Presley's Exxon credit card, one of his hats, and a lock of the King's hair. Stop in for an ice cream cone and check out the collection.

EASTERN

WESTERN
KENTUCKY PARKS

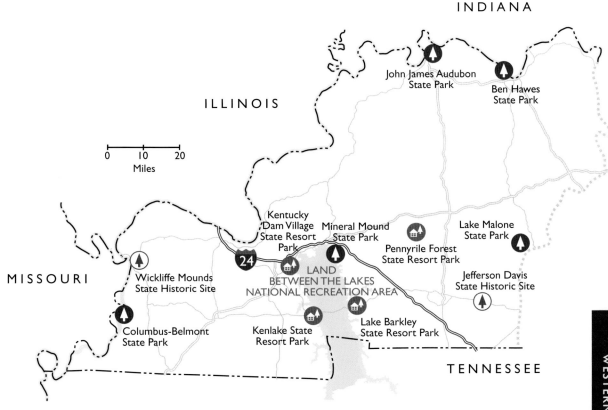

INDIANA

ILLINOIS

John James Audubon
State Park

Ben Hawes
State Park

0   10   20
Miles

MISSOURI

Kentucky
Dam Village
State Resort
Park

Mineral Mound
State Park

Lake Malone
State Park

Pennyrile Forest
State Resort Park

24

LAND
BETWEEN THE LAKES
NATIONAL RECREATION AREA

Wickliffe Mounds
State Historic Site

Jefferson Davis
State Historic Site

Columbus-Belmont
State Park

Kenlake State
Resort Park

Lake Barkley
State Resort Park

TENNESSEE

WESTERN

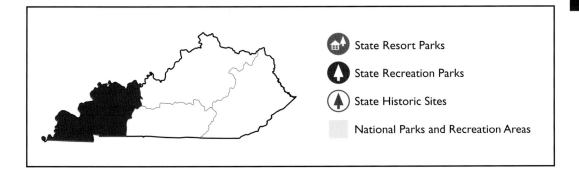

State Resort Parks

State Recreation Parks

State Historic Sites

National Parks and Recreation Areas

WESTERN STATE PARKS

- Year-round
- ○ Seasonal

		Park Acres	Lake Acres	Lodge and Dining Room	Cottages	Campground	✈: Airport; ▲: Air Camp
RESORT PARKS							
Kenlake	Hardin	1,795	128,807	●	●	○	
Kentucky Dam Village	Gilbertsville	1,351	128,807	●	●	●	✈ ▲
Lake Barkley	Cadiz	3,700	57,920	●	●	○	✈
Pennyrile Forest	Dawson Springs	863	56	●	●	○	
RECREATIONAL PARKS							
Ben Hawes	Owensboro	547					
Columbus-Belmont	Columbus	156				○	
John James Audubon	Henderson	692	40		●	●	
Lake Malone	Dunmore	349	788			○	
Mineral Mound	Eddyville	541	57,920				
HISTORIC SITES							
Jefferson Davis	Fairview	20					
Wickliffe Mounds	Wickliffe	26					

Golf (18-Hole, 9-Hole, or D: Disc Course)	Marina (L: Boat Launch Only)	Rental Boats	Swimming (P: Outdoor Pool, I: Indoor Pool, S: Slide, B: Beach)	Trails (Miles)	Riding Stables (○: Equestrian Trails)	Mountain Biking	Tennis Courts	Miniature Golf	Playgrounds	Picnic Area	Museum or Nature Center	Recreation/Interpretation Program
9	●	○	P	2			●		●	●		●
18	●	○	P/B		○		●		●	●		●
18	●	●	P/I/B	9		●	●		●	●	●	●
18		○	P/B	23			●	○	●	●		●
18				5		●			●	●		
	L			0.5				○	●	●	○	
9		○		6.5		●			●	●	●	●
	L		B	1.75					●	●		○
18	L								●			
									●	●	○	
				0.1					●	●		

177

BEN HAWES STATE PARK

400 Boothfield Road
Owensboro, KY 42301-9273
(270) 687-7134
http://www.parks.ky.gov/findparks/recparks/bh/
547 acres

BEN HAWES WAS a mayor of Owensboro, a city four miles to the east of this park. Ben Hawes State Park is a popular destination for the region's golfers, since they can choose to play all 18 holes of the park's centerpiece course or get in a quick round with a 9-hole configuration. The front 9 are fairly flat, too, while the back 9 are tucked among hilly, wooded terrain.

The wooded portion of the park, southwest of the golf course, contains a four-mile network of interconnected, looping trails. Some of these pass along deep depressions like large, hollowed-out ditches. There is a reason for the curious landforms. The land on which the park is situated was part of the George H. Rudy Mine, actively worked until the middle of the last century. It was one among several in the area that provided the energy for nearby Owensboro, literally fueling the city's growth.

If you follow the meandering trails through the woods to the park's southwestern-most corner, you will come to the remains of several mine buildings crouching beneath the trees. The state parks system has plans to incorporate the nine structures, including a mule barn, sawmill, dynamite shack, and scale house, into a future mine history interpretive center. In the meantime, beaches and picnic tables are the only enhancements on the site.

Casual visitors usually do not make the trek to the mine site. Much more popular are the park's picnic pavilions and playground, all located just inside the entrance before you reach the golf course parking lot.

FACILITY DETAILS

Meeting Rooms: These are located in the two-story house, listed on the National Register of Historic Places, that was the home of the mine owner. A large porch makes a fine al fresco meeting space, weather permitting.

Pro shop: Golf equipment is available here for rental and purchase.

Facing page: The golf course at Ben Hawes State Park.

Trails: The Willet Trail, just under 1 mile, begins at the other side of the playground and loops back through the woods to the trailhead. All other trails, located at the opposite corner of the park, intersect and range in

length from 0.4 mile to almost 2 miles. Mountain bikes are allowed on the trails, too.

Other Recreation: The park has an archery range, a softball field, and basketball courts in addition to the picnic shelters and playground.

Special Events: Golf tournaments are held frequently.

MORE TO EXPLORE

Since you are just minutes from downtown Owensboro, indulge in a regional specialty, a barbecued chopped mutton sandwich, and take it to the park for a picnic. Either the Moonlite Bar-B-Q Inn at 2840 West Parrish Avenue, (270) 684-8143, or Old Hickory Pit Bar-B-Q at 338 Washington Avenue, (270) 926-9000, can dish up this delicacy to go.

Also, if you love bluegrass music, you must visit the International Bluegrass Music Museum located near the riverfront. For information, go to http://www.bluegrass-museum.org/.

WESTERN

COLUMBUS-BELMONT STATE PARK

350 Park Road
Columbus, KY 42032-0009
(270) 677-2327
http://www.parks.ky.gov/findparks/recparks/cb/
156 acres

ON SEPTEMBER 3, 1861, Confederate troops commanded by General Leonidas Polk captured a site overlooking the Mississippi River on the 180-foot bluffs at Columbus, Kentucky. Not satisfied with having gun emplacements to guard the river and blockade Union shipping, Polk ordered a giant iron chain stretched across the river. It was a secured by a six-ton anchor at the Confederate camp on the opposite bank at Belmont, Missouri. The Confederates dug in at Columbus, constructing massive earthen trenches, and prepared to control the river at their "Gibraltar of the West."

It must have seemed like a good idea at the time, but it did not work. The chain did not hold. And in spite of having 140 cannons trained on the river and a geographically superior strategic position, Polk's men were eventually

Picnic tables at Columbus-Belmont State Park are sheltered in the earthen trenches dug by Confederate troops during the Civil War.

outflanked by Union troops. On March 3, 1862, Columbus was returned to federal authority. The name of the general commanding the Union forces, who with this engagement claimed his first victory of the Civil War, was Ulysses S. Grant.

The site of the battle has been preserved at this park, where the peacefulness of the setting and the beautiful vistas up and down the river contrast sharply to the chaos that reigned here in the fall of 1861 and spring of 1862. But there are reminders.

The trenches dug by the Confederate troops are still visible, though they are now covered in grass, rather than being banks of mud. A centerpiece of the park is the giant anchor, attached to a length of the chain that blockaded the river. Each enormous link is larger than your foot.

Count on spending at least a couple of hours here, especially if you or a member of your party is a Civil War history buff. Signs around the park tell the story of the battle, and the museum has even more detailed information. After taking in all this information about destruction and death, it is a relief to sit for a while in the little Civilian Conservation Corps–built gazebo overlooking the Mississippi and watch the slow progress of the river barges.

FACILITY DETAILS

Campground: Many campers say that sites 23–31 in the 38-site campground are the best in the state. All sites have utilities hookups. The campground is located on a high bluff overlooking the Mississippi, and 3 sites have river views. Open seasonally.

Museum: A restored antebellum frame house overlooking the river that served as a Confederate hospital during the Civil War houses a state-of-the-art history museum. Many of the exhibits about the Battle of Belmont include letters and journal entries of the participants. History of the town of Columbus, relocated after a flood in 1927, is also included in exhibits. Open seasonally. Admission fee.

Conference Center: Two attractive meeting rooms with fireplaces are available in a small conference center.

Gift Shop: Several books about the Civil War in general and the Columbus-Belmont history in particular are available in the shop, along with a selection of Kentucky-crafted products. Open daily May–September and on weekends the rest of the year.

WESTERN

Trail: A wide, 0.5-mile trail snakes beneath mature hardwoods and through the earthen trenches.

Boating: There is a boat ramp for access to the Mississippi River.

Other Recreation: The CCC built wood and stone picnic shelters with large central fireplaces. They overlook the river. Other picnic tables and grills are scattered throughout the park, including a couple located in the trenches dug by the Confederate troops. There are also a seasonal miniature golf course, a snack bar, and a playground.

Special Event: Civil War Days (October).

MORE TO EXPLORE

The authoritative and comprehensive tactical account of the battle fought on the park site is Nathaniel Cheairs Hughes Jr.'s *The Battle of Belmont: Grant Strikes South* (University of North Carolina Press). It is sold in the park gift shop. And here is a bit of history trivia: After the British burned Washington, DC, in the War of 1812, the town of Iron Banks changed its name to Columbus and proposed that the nation's capital move there. That did not happen, of course, and the park is not named Iron Banks–Belmont.

A farmhouse that served as a Civil War hospital is now a history museum at Columbus-Belmont State Park.

WESTERN

JEFFERSON DAVIS
STATE HISTORIC SITE

U.S. Highway 68 East
Fairview, KY 42221-0157
(270) 889-6100
http://www.parks.ky.gov/findparks/histparks/jd/
20 acres

A COMBINATION OF flat farmland and small subdivisions dominates the scenery on either side of U.S. Highway 68 near Hopkinsville. This is pretty typical of western Kentucky landscape in general, but as you approach Fairview, there are two striking anomalies.

The first is that you will frequently pass or meet black, horse-drawn buggies moving along the roadside at a fraction of the speed of other vehicles. There is a large Amish community here. The second is a tall gray obelisk piercing the sky on the south side of the highway, an engineering achievement in striking contrast to the low-tech ways of the buggy drivers over whom it looms.

The monument honors Jefferson Davis, president of the Confederate States of America, who was born on this site on June 3, 1808. Just over eight months later and less than 100 miles to the northeast, Abraham Lincoln was born. Leaders of both sides of the Civil War were natives of the border state of Kentucky.

While visitors will know Davis as the president of the Confederacy, many may not realize that he was a graduate of West Point, both a U.S. congressman and U.S. senator from Mississippi, secretary of war under President Franklin Pierce, and, until her premature death from malaria only three months after their wedding, husband to Knox Taylor, daughter of President Zachary Taylor.

These biographical details and more are on display in the visitor center. There is also information about the history and construction of the monument, which was commissioned by a group of Confederate Civil War veterans and built with a combination of money raised by the United Daughters of the Confederacy and an appropriation from the Kentucky General Assembly. It was completed in 1924, 35 years after Davis's death, when the site also became a part of the state parks system. That public money was contributed to a monument to someone whose citizenship was revoked for his part in the Civil War has stirred some amount of controversy ever since.

Facing page: An elevator takes visitors to an observation room at the top of the 351-foot obelisk at the Jefferson Davis State Historic Site.

WESTERN

184

Visitors can ride an elevator to the top of the 351-foot-tall monument, the world's tallest concrete obelisk and the United States' fifth-tallest monument. The panoramic view from the top is more than fair.

FACILITY DETAILS

Visitor Center: Exhibits in the center recount Davis's life and career and the history of the Confederate States of America's association with Kentucky, including information about Confederate regiments that were organized in the state. A short DVD about Davis provides a good introduction to the site. Open from May through October.

Gift Shop: As you might expect, there are many Civil War–related products here, including flags, models, figurines, and even chess sets. Book selection leans heavily toward a southern perspective on the war.

Recreation: The park has two modern picnic shelters and a small playground.

Special Events: Jefferson Davis Birthday Commemoration (June).

MORE TO EXPLORE

For another aspect of area history, visit the Trail of Tears Commemorative Park, located in Hopkinsville, about 10 miles west of the Jefferson Davis State Historic Site. It is on a portion of land that is one of the few known campgrounds for the infamous Trail of Tears, along which, in 1838 and 1839, Cherokees were forced to walk from their homelands in the Carolinas to "Indian territory" in Oklahoma. Two chiefs who died on the journey, White Path and Fly Smith, are buried here. A national powwow takes place here every year on the weekend after Labor Day. For more information, go to http://www.trailoftears.org/.

WESTERN

JOHN JAMES AUDUBON STATE PARK

3100 U.S. Highway 41 North
Henderson, KY 42419-0576
(270) 826-2247
http://www.parks.ky.gov/findparks/recparks/au/
692 acres; 40 lake acres

A GREAT BLUE HERON stands statue-still in shallow water at the lakeshore, alert to the movement of fish. In the canopy of trees overhead,
warblers dart about in the highest branches, while woodpeckers, from the
diminutive downy to the crow-sized pileated, drill the trunks for insects.

This is just a snapshot of the bird life visitors can find at John James
Audubon State Park, encompassing more than 700 acres near the Ohio
River. America's most famous wildlife artist lived nearby and explored this
area from 1810 to 1819. Its woods, bluffs, and ponds were rich sources for his
studies and paintings of birds and mammals.

The park is located along a major migratory route, so avid and even
casual ornithologists are today rewarded with a seasonally changing variety
of bird life. A checklist available at the park's office lists nearly 170 species.
Audubon would have seen most of these, though changes in habitat have
allowed some new ones, such as the house finch, to arrive. Other species

Sunset on the
recreational lake.

familiar to him, including the ivory-billed woodpecker and the whooping crane, are gone.

In his *Ornithological Biography,* the artist described one bird so common that it seems impossible that none is left. In the autumn of 1813, Audubon made a trip on horseback from his house in Henderson to Louisville. Along the way, he encountered flocks of passenger pigeons:

> The air was literally filled with Pigeons; the light of the noon-day was obscured as by an eclipse; the dung fell in spots, not unlike melting flakes of snow; and the continued buzz of wings had a tendency to lull my senses to repose.

The French chateau museum and nature center. Birds nest in the tower niches.

Today, it is hard to imagine the vast clouds of these birds encountered by Audubon and his contemporaries. The species is, like the dodo, famously extinct. A combination of unchecked hunting (pigeon pie, described by numerous frontiersmen as "delicious," was apparently the fast food of the American frontier) and habitat destruction led to its demise.

But Audubon's legacy of careful observations and, of course, his detailed paintings of the wildlife he encountered in Kentucky are celebrated at the park, including in the museum housing one of the largest collections of Audubon art and artifacts in the world.

The building itself is a knockout. Who would expect to find a slate-and-stone Norman chateau, complete with a turret outfitted with niches in the bricks for nesting birds, in the middle of a Kentucky forest? (Birds do indeed use the niches; look for the straw and twigs sticking out of the openings.) But that is exactly what the park's main building is. The architectural inspiration was Audubon's French heritage. In addition to exhibits about Audubon's life and work, it houses an art gallery, classrooms, a wildlife viewing station, and a gift shop.

The museum—and the guest cottages with working fireplaces by one of the park's small lakes—were built in 1938 with the skilled, Depression-era labor of President Franklin Roosevelt's Works Progress Administration (WPA) and Civilian Conservation Corps (CCC). Cobbled courtyards, retaining walls, and park office buildings, also built by the CCC, match the main building's architecture and complement the beauty of the natural setting.

Spring may be the best time of year to visit the park. Carpets of wildflowers, including bloodroot, trout lily, trillium, and blue-eyed mary, bloom on the forest floor. Almost 340 acres within the park make up a dedicated Kentucky state nature preserve, so designated for the many rare wildflower and fern, as well as bird, species. Checklists of the 280 species of wildflowers as well as of trees, shrubs, and ferns are available at the park office.

And of course, in spring, birds

Blue-eyed mary blooms at John James Audubon State Park in late March and early April.

WESTERN

A male rose-breasted grosbeak at the wildlife observation room. This species is a spring and fall visitor at John James Audubon State Park.

on the move stop by. Only in spring and fall can the rose-breasted grosbeak be seen in Kentucky. There is no mistaking the male, a robin-sized bird with a bright splash of reddish pink feathers on his chest. The buff-colored female is less spectacular, though no less attractive, with a beak that glows pale pink during the spring mating season.

A great place to see the birds, wielding their eponymous seed-cracking beaks, is through the plateglass windows overlooking an outdoor collection of feeders at the nature center.

If the day is fine, set off along the paved Warbler Road with your binoculars, checklists, and field guides. This road gives access to 6.5 miles of wooded trails. The forest has a timeless atmosphere, perhaps because of the large beech trees found throughout it. Most of the hiking is easy to moderate, though the hilly, 1.6-mile Back Country Trail—accessed via the Wilderness Lake Trail—is best enjoyed by experienced hikers. The CCC very thoughtfully erected stone and wood shelters at strategic resting points along the steeper parts of the park's trails.

FACILITY DETAILS

Museum: Features a series of displays about Audubon's rags-to-riches-to-rags-again life. A life-size diorama shows the artist at work in his studio, complete with taxidermied specimens like the ones he shot and posed for his paintings. Family possessions include the silver service Audubon bought for his long-suffering and beloved wife Lucy on a trip to London, replacing one that had to be sold during leaner times to raise cash. One exhibit shows how the famous books of the naturalist's paintings were made. Right by this is a copy of the famous double elephant folio of *The Birds of America*. It is displayed under glass and illuminated so you can examine every line of the colored prints. Museum staff members turn the page every once in a while, so on a return visit, you will have a new one to examine. The edition's name came from its great size, designed so that the largest birds among the 435 species depicted could be painted exactly life-size. Even that device still left the artist having to paint birds such as the greater flamingo and trumpeter swan with their long necks bent at funny angles. The collection includes copies of many other editions of *The Birds of America* as well as Audubon's series of mammals, *The Viviparous Quadrupeds of North America*. There is an entrance fee.

Nature Center: Large circular viewing room with plate glass windows from which you can view birds at feeding stations. An exhibit about bird anatomy, behavior, and ecology is found in a room next door.

Gift Shop: Excellent selection of field guides, as well as books about John James Audubon. Also, cards re-creating famous paintings and limited edition prints of selected paintings.

Art Gallery: Rotating exhibits of work by living wildlife artists.

Classrooms and Meeting Facilities: Park staff give a variety of interpretive programs throughout the year to both the public and visiting school groups. Rooms in the museum building can be rented for meetings accommodating up to 150.

WESTERN

Cottages: The five one-bedroom cottages around the recreational lake have working fireplaces. Numbers 101 and 102 have the best lake views. One two-bedroom ADA-compliant cottage of more recent vintage is also available.

Campground: Located by the entrance off heavily traveled U.S. Highway 41, the campground is not exactly bucolic. But it is shady, and campers using its 69 sites, all with utilities hookups, have access to a bathhouse, picnic tables and grills, and a playground.

Trails: There are eight, ranging from the 0.25-mile Museum Trail that loops behind the museum to the 1.6-mile Back Country Trail that involves a total of 3.3 miles of walking since you have to get to it from other trails.

Fishing: Fishing is permitted on the 28-acre recreational lake for catfish, bluegill, largemouth bass, and other species stocked by the state. No fishing is allowed on the 12-acre Wilderness Lake. It is strictly for the birds and other wildlife, including turtles basking in the sun on logs.

Recreation: Nine-hole golf course, tennis courts, picnic shelters, playground, paddleboats for the recreational lake in season.

Special Events: Bird Migration Walk (May), Creative Arts and Homegrown Music Festival (May), Monarch Migration Tag (September), Adult Artists Workshops (several times a year).

MORE TO EXPLORE

Richard Rhodes's excellent, award-winning biography, *John James Audubon: The Making of an American* (Vintage Books), is highly recommended reading if you want to know more about Audubon's life and times. To read the artist's own words, *Audubon: Writings and Drawings* (Library of America) is the best one-volume collection. Both are available in the park's gift shop.

KENLAKE STATE RESORT PARK

542 Kenlake Road
Hardin, KY 42048-9737
(270) 474-2211 or (800) 325-0143
http://www.parks.ky.gov/findparks/resortparks/kl/
1,795 acres; 128,807 lake acres

MUSIC ENTHUSIASTS KNOW Kentucky as the home of bluegrass and the location of the Country Music Highway, a route in eastern Kentucky along which many stars were born. Yet another music genre reigns supreme every summer when thousands of fans flock to Kenlake State Resort Park for the annual Hot August Blues Festival.

For the better part of a steamy summer weekend, the park's lakeside amphitheater reverberates with the amplified strains of such blues favorites as B. B. King's signature tune "The Thrill Is Gone" and Blind Willie McTell's "Statesboro Blues." A large banner hanging from the side of the stage reads, "Welcome to the Kenlake Hot August Blues Festival—Warning: The Blues Is Contagious." The enthusiastic crowd certainly catches a severe case.

At the end of each number, shouts and applause break out from dancers just below the stage as well as from the listeners who have brought their

There is a high audience participation rate during the festival.

The annual Hot August Blues Festival takes place on the stage overlooking Kentucky Lake.

own lawn chairs to set up on the concrete amphitheater rows. More fans lounge in folding canvas chairs or lie on blankets under trees on the hillside. Out on Kentucky Lake, hundreds of houseboats and smaller craft are anchored so their occupants can hear the music, and boat horns hoot appreciation after each song. Both the infectious music and the contents of beer-stocked coolers inspire the enthusiasm.

In short, if you are a blues fan, the Hot August Blues Festival is an event you will want to put on your calendar. But that is only one of Kenlake's many attractions.

When it opened in 1952, Kentucky Lake State Park (as it was then called) was advertised as the state's "first modern resort park." Driving up the tree-lined drive to the white stucco park hotel, you may think you are caught in a time warp. The place looks so 1950s that you expect to see women wearing gloves and pillbox hats and men wearing open-necked shirts and pleated trousers strolling around the colorful flower gardens surrounding the building. When I visited, a mental image of James Stewart and Doris Day popped so vividly to mind that I started humming "Que Sera, Sera" under my breath as I parked the car.

The rooms in the hotel have been updated. Even though there are interior corridors, it is run along the lines of other state park lodges. Do not expect room service. But there are amenities. A wide lawn slopes down from the gardens to the shore of the lake, the perfect place for a quiet, after-dinner walk. The swimming pool overlooks the lake, too.

Beautifully designed and meticulously maintained gardens are of such quality that Kenlake belongs to the American Association of Botanical Gardens and Arboreta. Many patios and balconies overlook the flowerbeds, as do the hotel dining room and meeting rooms. Butterflies and bees dart among the blooms. One special garden is pleasing not just to the eye. A sign invites guests to smell and touch the rosemary, lavender, lemon balm, and other fragrant herbs planted in a border near one backdoor of the hotel.

If you venture much beyond the hotel area, you will probably do so by car. The amphitheater and tennis center are a mile from the hotel, as is the campground. If you are in a mood for exploring, a unique piece of the park history can be seen off Highway 68, past the campground entrance, a little over a mile from the hotel.

Several buildings remain on what were the grounds of Cherokee State Park. Since the Kenlake resort opened during the era of racial segregation in Kentucky, it was for whites only. But a park was also created for the exclusive use of African Americans. It was the only such park in Kentucky and one of only a few such facilities in the United States. You can still see the lodge that contained a dining hall seating 200. The boat dock and fishing dock remain, as do some of the 10 cottages that once could be rented. Unfortunately, instead of simply being added to the overall accommodations at Kenlake after desegregation, Cherokee State Park was closed. There has been some interest in restoring the park; check Kenlake's Web site for updates about its status.

FACILITY DETAILS

Hotel: It has 48 rooms, a gift shop, and the 182-seat Aurora Landing Restaurant. A large shaded patio at the entrance has furniture on which you can sit and enjoy the gardens if you are on the lookout for friends arriving at the hotel.

WESTERN

Boaters listen to the blues.

Cottages: There are 34 cottages in three different areas of the park. Some of the ones near the hotel are right on the lakeshore and have excellent views of the water. They have one, two, or three bedrooms, so they can accommodate a couple or a party.

Campground: All 90 sites in this large campground are equipped with utilities hookups. Open from mid-March to mid-November.

Tennis Center: The park has a certified tennis referee on staff, and the game is a draw for park visitors. The center has four indoor courts, with locker rooms. These are open in the winter, from November 1 to April 1. Four outdoor courts are open year-round.

Trails: A short path connects two looping trails through the wooded portion of the park, Cherokee and Chickasaw, so you can enjoy a good two-mile hike. A short lakefront trail from the hotel passes behind some of the park cottages.

Fishing and Boating: This is the largest human-created lake in the eastern United States, so fishing is naturally a very popular activity. There are boat slips for your craft, and you can fish along the shore. The lodge staff can connect you with a professional fish guide who will take you on half-day or day-long excursions. Fishing boats, pontoon boats, and jet skis can be rented.

Golf Course: A nine-hole course, with a pro shop, is located at the western side of the park.

Other Recreation: Picnic shelters and tables and playgrounds are located throughout the park. There is also a basketball court between the hotel and the lake.

Special Events: Eagle Weekend (February), Kentucky Lake Bluegrass Festival (June), Hot August Blues Festival. Many tennis tournaments and fishing events are held throughout the year.

MORE TO EXPLORE

Kenlake is one of three resort parks bordering the Land Between the Lakes National Recreation Area. (Lake Barkley and Kentucky Dam Village are the others.) Created when Kentucky Lake and Lake Barkley were formed in the 1940s, the 170,000-acre peninsula, known as LBL for short, is a wildlife management area. It contains several significant historic sites, a planetarium, and a 19th-century demonstration working farm. For an overview of the opportunities here, including hunting and backcountry hiking and camping, go to http://www.lbl.org/.

The 15-minute drive from Kenlake Park is the shortest from the three LBL area parks to what I think is the most fascinating feature of Land Between the Lakes, the Elk and Bison Prairie. Visit it at dawn, when there are the fewest visitors. Your car has to pass through a gate in the high fence surrounding the preserve, and then you are on a three-mile road that loops through the hilly prairie. Go very slowly. An elk could

A pair of bison bulls engage in a dominance duel at the Elk and Bison Prairie.

WESTERN

Two bull elks compete for mates at the Elk and Bison Prairie.

be browsing on tree branches just a few feet from the roadside. During the mating season in October and early November, the haunting, insistent cry of the bulls (called bugling) echoes throughout the preserve. You may even see a pair of males literally head-to-head in territorial combat, their antlers locked together, each pushing the other until one yields.

The herd of huge, shaggy bison may wander across the road and surround your car. Crack your windows and you can smell them. Do not reach a hand out to pet them. They may look like shaggy cattle, but they are wild animals.

It may take several passes around the loop before you see any animals, but patience is usually rewarded. It is a fabulous experience, like going on a wildlife safari in Kentucky. Take your camera. You may see bald eagles, wild turkeys, and bluebirds, too.

KENTUCKY DAM VILLAGE
STATE RESORT PARK

113 Administration Drive
Gilbertsville, KY 42044-0069
(270) 362-4271 or (800) 325-0146
http://www.parks.ky.gov/findparks/resortparks/kd/
1,351 acres; 128,807 lake acres

> The clouds were torn by the wind, and the red sunset slashed the West. Seeing the sudden gleam in the gloom Bilbo looked round. He gave a great cry: he had seen a sight that made his heart leap, dark shapes small yet majestic against the distant glow. "The Eagles! The Eagles!" he shouted. "The Eagles are coming!"—J. R. R. Tolkein, *The Hobbit*

An American bald eagle soars over Kentucky Lake.

IT WAS NOT in Middle Earth but in western Kentucky, at lunchtime on a January Saturday, when a shout, "The eagles! Look, eagles!" echoed around the park lodge dining room. The excited voice belonged not to a hobbit but to a park ranger at Kentucky Dam Village State Resort Park.

Everyone within hearing rushed to the windows. Below the lodge, just above the surface of Kentucky Lake, two American bald eagles soared and circled. One dropped like a missile and rose with a wriggling fish in its talons. Both birds made for the shoreline trees, long wings beating with powerful strokes. It was quite a show, the best view of the birds I got all weekend.

Thanks to the images on coins, government seals, and postage stamps, we all know the fierce, proud profile of the American bald eagle, the nation's symbol. After experiencing the park's annual Gathering of Eagles weekend, you will have another, far less formal, image of the birds. On van outings into the Land Between the Lakes National Recreation Area and boat excursions along the shore of Kentucky Lake, you will get lots of practice looking for the telltale white heads of the eagles as they perch in tree branches, dotting the limbs like oversize, alabaster Christmas ornaments. Spot the white, then train your binoculars on the image, and you will see the hooked beak

Eagle spotters are bundled against the cold during the Kentucky Dam Village State Resort Park Gathering of Eagles boat ride on Kentucky Lake.

and the formidable talons. They are truly handsome birds.

While state and federal naturalists have recorded several pairs of nesting eagles that stay in the area year-round, the best chance of seeing the birds in large numbers is during the winter, when they come from points north to Kentucky Lake and Lake Barkley. Here they can fish in water located far enough south that it does not freeze. Plus, with the leaves off the trees, the eagles are easier to see. Sometimes, they even put on a show like the one I was lucky enough to see at lunch.

Going out on Saturday to look for the birds is just part of the weekend. The Friday evening before, naturalists from the U.S. Forest Service give a presentation on eagle biology and behavior they call Eagle Basics 101. Among the fascinating bird facts are the following:

- Eagles have wing spans of up to eight feet and can weigh as much as 20 pounds.
- Talon strength is 1,000 pounds of pressure per square inch. (Once caught, fish do not escape.)
- Kentucky Lake and Lake Barkley have a combined undeveloped shoreline of 300 miles, providing an enormous number of perching and nesting sites for the birds, whose diets consist of 75 percent fish.

While the eagle weekend has become a major event at Kentucky Dam Village, that is by no means the park's only attraction. Its configuration is unique in the state park system.

Many of the buildings date from the late 1930s and early 1940s, when the Tennessee Valley Authority was building Kentucky Dam. It literally formed a village, complete with cottages for the workers, an auditorium, and its own electrical, water, and sewage systems. You will also notice the park's post office, located across the road from the entrance to the lodge. Kentucky Dam Village is the only Kentucky state park with its own post office.

The cottages, some in wooded areas, others near the lake or golf course, are excellent retreats and especially suited for extended stays. A golfing outing would be ideal. The lake, of course, has a multitude of recreational opportunities. Birders will see many, many shorebird species in addition to the eagle.

WESTERN

FACILITY DETAILS

Lodges: The 72 Village Inn Lodge rooms were renovated in 2006–2007 with updates that include art deco details and designer fabrics. Most look out onto the lake. Also updated was the smaller, 14-room Village Green Inn next to the golf course. The entire Village Green Inn can be rented for a group. The main lodge contains the Harbor Lights Restaurant, which overlooks the lake, dam, and marina. Its swimming pool is for lodge and cottages guests only.

Cottages: The arrangement of the cottages is a strong reminder of the park's name. Many of the 48 cottages on the west side of Highway 641 date from the construction of Kentucky Dam, when they provided housing for the workers. These have been renovated, and more modern cottages, many with wraparound porches, have been built overlooking the golf course. Twenty two-story executive cottages are arranged in the woods on a road leading off the entrance to the boat dock.

Campground: The 219-site campground is literally on the other side of the tracks. The road from the rest of the park property goes over a railroad crossing. All sites have utilities hookups, and there are a grocery, playground, and recreation pavilion. The boat basin is on the Tennessee River. If you come to Kentucky Dam Village in your private plane, there is an air camp, too.

One of the newer cottages near the golf course.

WESTERN

Sailboats at the marina.

Airport: A 4,000-foot paved, lighted airstrip within the park is 1.5 miles from the main lodge. Aviation fuel is not available.

Cypress Wetland: A remnant of the cypress wetland that used to dominate this region of the state is preserved within the park, just off Forest Nursery Road. Bring your binoculars or spotting scope to the observation area to see a variety of waterfowl including herons, osprey, cormorants, and kingfishers. A pair of nesting bald eagles have settled here, too.

Fishing and Boating: Obviously, these are major activities for park visitors. Fish in the lake include largemouth, smallmouth, Kentucky, and white bass, plus sauger, crappie, bluegill, and channel and blue catfish. The marina has overnight dockage, rental fishing boats, pontoon boats, ski boats, and pedal boats. Rentals available from March 1 to October 31.

Golf Course: This was the first of the park system's signature series courses and is laid out over sloping, but not hilly, terrain. It is an 18-hole, par 72 course and plays 6,704 yards from the back tees. The pro shop is fully equipped with equipment and carts.

Other Recreation: Horseback riding stables, tennis courts, and a variety of planned recreation activities. A sandy beach for swimming is located just below the lodge.

Sunset over Kentucky Lake from the grounds of Kentucky Dam Village State Resort Park.

Special Events: Gathering of Eagles (January), Buffalo Dinner and Native American Heritage Day (April), Spring Arts and Crafts Festival (May), Good Ole USA Days (July), Fall Arts and Crafts Show (October).

MORE TO EXPLORE

When the Army Corps of Engineers created Kentucky Lake and Lake Barkley in the 1940s, the farms and most of the towns in the area that became Land Between the Lakes were abandoned, and the peninsula is now a national recreation area. But at the very northern tip of LBL, you will find the town of Grand Rivers. It is just a few minutes' drive from the park and offers several shops and restaurants of the home-style cooking variety. Keep in mind that Livingston County is dry, so you cannot enjoy a glass of anything stronger than iced tea with your meal. For details about the town's attractions, go to http://www.grandrivers.com/.

WESTERN

LAKE BARKLEY STATE RESORT PARK

3500 State Park Road
Cadiz, KY 42211-0790
(270) 924-1131 or (800) 325-1708
http://www.parks.ky.gov/findparks/resortparks/lb/
3,700 acres; 57,920 lake acres

A CANAL CONNECTS Lake Barkley to Kentucky Lake, forming the largest engineered body of water on earth. Together, the lakes have just over 1,000 miles of shoreline and almost 187,000 acres of water. No wonder they attract birds migrating along the Mississippi Valley flyway. The presence of wintering American bald eagles in the area is well known. But on trips here in spring and fall, you will spy birds not commonly associated with Kentucky.

I was having breakfast in the lodge dining room on a clear, early November morning when I was intrigued to see a line of large white birds, wings edged black, flying in an undulating, single-file line over the lake. It was almost as if they were choreographed. Even their wings beat at the same

White pelicans stop off at Lake Barkley during their spring and fall migrations.

time. Then they flew close enough that their long, orange bills were obvious. The American white pelicans were paying their semiannual visit to Lake Barkley.

Forget all the silly cartoon pelicans you have seen. The real birds are wonderfully graceful. I spent the better part of an afternoon watching a flock glide around the surface of the lake, in a small inlet just below the lodge. They were fishing. Every few minutes, one of the pelicans would tip bottom-up to submerge its head in the water, then rock back upright. Backlit by the sun, a wriggling fish was briefly visible in the bird's pouch until, with one swallow, it was gone.

Eventually, a boat carrying two human anglers arrived, and the noise of the outboard engine prompted the pelicans to take to the air. I noticed another craft far out on the lake that was about to take off, too. The park has a landing strip for airplanes with wheels, but the long, smooth lake surface is also used by seaplanes for takeoffs and landings. A bright red plane was taxiing out onto the water from the marina. It turned, gained speed, and lifted into the air as the line of pelicans flew into the distance, too.

From the vantage of the lodge, it is common to see great blue herons and various gulls. Woodpeckers and songbirds frequent the mature hardwoods surrounding the building. But the most conspicuous wildlife in the park must be white-tailed deer. They are everywhere—grazing by the roadsides, in lawns by cottages, and out on the golf course. I must have seen dozens of them before I spotted a single squirrel.

Obviously wildlife watchers will have a great time here. But the park also has more kinds of recreational opportunities than any other in the state system, and the lodge accommodations are elegant.

FACILITY DETAILS

Lodge: Edward Durrell Stone designed the Lake Barkley Lodge, which has 120 rooms and 4 suites. The central building has a beautiful, clubby lobby furnished with upholstered sofas and wing chairs. A display case at the head of the stairs leading to the dining room contains personal effects of Alban Barkley, including a walking stick and hat. The Graves County native was a U.S. senator and congressman from Kentucky and vice president of the United States under Harry Truman. Soaring spaces crisscrossed with wooden beams are open to the sky and the lake. Three and a half acres of glass were used for windows and skylights. The rooms are located in arms extending from either side of the central lodge and arch along the lakeshore.

WESTERN

They are furnished beautifully, too. Jacquard sheets on the beds are the most luxurious in the parks system. The lodge restaurant has three-story walls of glass, a central fireplace, and 400 seats. There is a large game room on the lowest floor, as well as several meeting spaces on several levels. The park's swimming pool is situated between the front of the lodge and the lake. The much smaller Little River Lodge, with 10 rooms and 1 suite, is tucked away in a wooded valley a short drive from the main lodge. It can be rented as a whole for a family or group.

The lodge swimming pool overlooks Lake Barkley.

Facing page: The lobby of the lodge at Lake Barkley State Resort Park is an inviting space.

Cottages: Nine two-bedroom, two-bathroom cottages with lake or woodland views have screened porches or decks. If you have always wanted to spend the night in a log cabin, the park has four of them. (Each with two bedrooms, they are considerably bigger and more comfortable that the one in which Abe Lincoln was born.) The backs of the cabins overlook woods.

Campground: The campground has 78 sites with utilities hookups. Numbers 37–53 have views of the lake, and several have wooden decks where you can picnic. (Some campers use these as frameworks for tents.) The wooded campground also has a boat ramp for campers' exclusive use. Open from mid-March to mid-November.

Airport: Three miles from the lodge, near the park's entrance, is a 4,800-foot paved, lighted airstrip. Aviation fuel is not available.

Fitness Center: If the weather is too nasty for hiking, you can always work out (or pamper yourself) in this state-of-the-art facility. It has Nautilus machines, stationary bicycles, a free-weight room, leverage equipment, a racquetball court, tanning beds, a sauna, a steam room, a whirlpool, and a heated indoor swimming pool. There is also a staff massage therapist. Some

WESTERN

facilities are free to park guests and others are offered for a daily fee; ask at the lodge desk.

Trails: The park has five marked trails from 0.3 mile to just over 2.5 miles long. Many interconnect so you can design longer hikes. Bear in might that the terrain is pretty rugged, so even the relatively short Lena Madesin Phillips Self-Guided Interpretive Trail (0.75 mile) takes a good 45 minutes to walk. It is an excellent introduction to the ecosystems of the park, since it takes you along the lake, through the woods, and even over a swing bridge. Booklets describing numbered stations are available.

Fishing and Boating: The marina has 112 covered slips, 60 open slips, and a launching ramp. Fishing boats, pontoon boats, and ski boats can be rented. Among the lake sport fish are crappie, bluegill, and largemouth, white, and Kentucky bass. Facilities are open year-round. Contact the marina at (270) 924-9954.

Golf Course: Half of the holes on the 18-hole Boots Randolph Golf Course have play involving a spring-fed stream that meanders along the tree-lined fairways. The most difficult hole is reputedly number 6. It has a 90-degree dogleg fairway and is par five.

Other Recreation: A public beach with a volleyball court and a trap range across the road from the golf course are seasonal. Two lighted tennis courts are near the lodge. A large picnic pavilion is located near the lake on the opposite shore from the lodge. The park has a recreation director who organizes activities throughout the year.

Special Events: Eagle Watch Weekend (January), Backpacking Hikes and Workshops (several times a year).

MORE TO EXPLORE

A great way to view the waterfowl and other wildlife at Lake Barkley is on one of the naturalist-led Eco Boat Trips. The maximum number of passengers is just six, and you cruise on the lake in a nifty 23-foot boat. Three different daily tours are offered in late afternoon and evening, June through October. Spring for the 90-minute sunset tour that goes to the osprey nests. And do not forget to bring your binoculars. Lifejackets are provided. For information or to book a tour, call the park.

LAKE MALONE STATE PARK

331 State Route Road 8001
Dunmore, KY 42339-0093
(270) 657-2111
http://www.parks.ky.gov/findparks/recparks/lm/
349 acres; 788 lake acres

UNLESS YOU STRIKE OUT on the Laurel Trail, which snakes along the park's wooded bluffs, or take a boat out onto the water, you will miss the most dramatic feature of Lake Malone, the 50-foot-high sandstone cliffs that form much of the lake's southern shoreline.

This is a pocket-size park by state system standards, and it is somewhat tucked out of the way. The park is about halfway between Central City and Russellville. You have to take several secondary roads for about 20 miles from the nearest four-lane highways. Combined with its small size, this may be why this is one of the system's quieter parks. It is also a good one for a scenic, not too taxing walk, since the trails are pretty flat. The lake and park are named in honor of W. C. Malone and his wife, who, in the early 1960s, donated 200 acres (and sold another 75 acres) to the state for what would become the park.

FACILITY DETAILS

Campground: Tent camping at 30 primitive sites and 25 RV and camper sites with utilities hookups. The campground has picnic shelters, tables and grills, and a playground.

Trails: The Laurel Trail is a 1.5-mile loop from which you can see the sandstone bluffs of the park and rock shelters once used by American Indians. The hardwood forest through which it winds contains mountain laurel, holly, and dogwoods, as well as mature

A campground playground at Lake Malone State Park.

Sandstone cliffs near Lake Malone.

hickories and oaks. A walk along the 0.25-mile Wildflower Trail is best in the spring.

Fishing and Boating: A boat ramp on the northwest shore of the lake gives access to the water and fishing for redear sunfish, catfish, bluegill, largemouth bass, and other species stocked by the state.

Swimming: The lake has a sandy beach and a beach house located near the boat ramp. You can splash about with a fine view of the wooded cliffs from the water. Open seasonally.

Special Events: Check with the park about occasional guided nature walks and other activities.

MORE TO EXPLORE

If you are not a camper, a fascinating place to stay within an hour of the park is the Shaker Tavern Bed and Breakfast in South Union. It is part of a restored Shaker community that houses the largest collection of western Shaker furniture and artifacts in the United States. Go to http://www.shakermuseum.com/ for details.

MINERAL MOUND STATE PARK

8 Finch Lane
Eddyville, KY 42038
(270) 388-3673
http://www.parks.ky.gov/findparks/recparks/mm/
541 acres; 57,920 lake acres

MINERAL MOUND STATE PARK is home to one of the parks system's signature series 18-hole golf courses. The front 9 holes are laid out through the wooded hills of the park. Many of the back 9 skirt the shore of Lake Barkley, including number 11, which plays over an inlet of the lake. You would think that losing your ball in the trees or the water would be the greatest hazard here. But actually, hole 15 is the tricky one. It is the fox hole.

When you check in at the pro shop, look behind the counter. You will see a framed, slightly blurry photo of a red fox running across grass. Look closer, and you will discover it has a golf ball in its mouth. The shop staff

A red fox family, whose members have been known to steal a ball now and then, lives on the golf course at Mineral Mound State Park.

members are happy to relate the story of the fox family that lives at the course. The animals can often be seen in the early morning walking around the clubhouse. They seem to be attracted to the smell of coffee, and they apparently view golf balls as their special toys. Do not be surprised if one of them stands by, covetously eyeing your ball, while you are trying to hit it. You and your golfing companions should probably agree on a vulpine mulligan before you tee off.

In addition to the interactive wildlife, Mineral Mound State Park has a pretty interesting history. The property was once the farm of Willis B. Machen, who was a road and bridge builder, lawyer, member of the Kentucky General Assembly, and U.S. congressman. His granddaughter, Zelda Sayre, visited frequently when she was child. She would become one of the best-known figures of the Jazz Age as a short-story writer and wife of author F. Scott Fitzgerald.

The park is named for Machen's mansion, which he built on a hill overlooking the Cumberland River. During the Civil War, Machen served in the Confederate Congress and flew a large Confederate flag on his property. This provocative show of the Stars and Bars drew cannon fire from a Union gunboat passing along the Cumberland that damaged the mansion. After the war, Machen and his family lived in Canada until he was pardoned by

Facing page: Fishing from the Lyon County boat ramp at Mineral Mound State Park.

WESTERN

The clubhouse and pro shop on the 18-hole golf course overlook Lake Barkley.

President Andrew Johnson for his role in the conflict. They then returned to Kentucky.

After Machen's death, dairy farmer George Catlett owned Mineral Mound until he sold it to R. S. Mason, who also farmed on the site until just after World War II. The house that had survived a 19th-century artillery attack caught fire early on the morning of February 3, 1947, and burned to the ground. Only the overgrown ruins of the foundation, visible along part of the golf course, remain.

FACILITY DETAILS

Clubhouse: The handsome, three-story clubhouse was finished in 2007. Painted cheerful yellow with white trim and a green roof, it has wraparound balconies with views of the lake where you can sit and sip a soft drink after your golf round. The clubhouse is also equipped with a snack bar and a pro shop. Carts, clubs, and any other needed equipment can be rented here.

Fishing and Boating: A boat ramp off the parking lot gives access to Lake Barkley. There is also a fishing pier from which you can cast your line.

Other Recreation: There are a couple of picnic tables near the water.

MORE TO EXPLORE

Adsmore House and Gardens, billed as a living house museum, is about half an hour from the park, in Princeton. Home to several generations of a wealthy local family, the rooms change settings with the seasons to illustrate life here in the years between 1901 and the Great War. The Web site is http://www.adsmore.org/.

WESTERN

PENNYRILE FOREST STATE RESORT PARK

20781 Pennyrile Lodge Road
Dawson Springs, KY 42408
(270) 797-3421 or (800) 325-1711
http://www.parks.ky.gov/findparks/resortparks/pf/
863 acres; 56 lake acres

AMERICAN PENNYROYAL *(Hedeoma pulegioides)* is a member of the mint family. It grows in pungent, foot-high patches and is usually more noticeable by scent than by sight until late summer. That is when its slender stalks are covered with tiny, pale purple flowers. When settlers arrived in western Kentucky, pennyroyal grew abundantly in sunny fields and open areas of woodlands. So the region, now known as the Pennyroyal, was named after the plant.

Today, botanists classify pennyroyal's distribution as infrequent. One of the few places wildflower lovers can find it is along the Pennyroyal Trail in Pennyrile Forest State Resort Park. ("Pennyroyal" with a Kentucky accent becomes "pennyrile." Local pronunciation won out in the naming of the park.) And in some ways, the park resembles the flower.

Compared to other state parks in the region, Pennyrile is small and inconspicuous. It is nestled inside the 15,331-acre Pennyrile State Forest, and you have to make a point of finding it. The state has thoughtfully provided signs along the route from the Western Kentucky Parkway exit to the park entrance. It is the park's small scale that makes it especially appealing if you are looking for a quiet getaway.

The 24-room stone lodge and eight of the park's cottages overlook the lake, which is ringed on all sides by wooded hills. Beautiful any time of the year, the woods and water combination is especially striking in the spring, when the hills are painted with the deep pink and bright white of redbuds and dogwoods, and in the fall, when the mixed hardwood forest leaves blaze red and gold.

A young angler shows off his catch from the lake at Pennyrile Forest State Resort Park.

Fishing in the early morning on Pennyrile Lake.

Mist rising from the lake in the early morning also makes Pennyrile Forest State Resort Park seem remote and secret. The stillness is barely disturbed by anglers out on the water at dawn, since only very small trolling motors are allowed. In fact, the scenery and the small size make the park's lake perfect for people-powered boats, such as canoes, kayaks, and paddleboats.

The outstanding recreation feature of the park is its 23-mile network of trails. They wind through a variety of terrains and habitats and range from easy to difficult. Even if you do not hike the moderately strenuous Pennyroyal Trail between July and September, when you can see the eponymous wildflower, it is still one of the most scenic walks. It overlooks the lake's beach, passes through oak-hickory stands before leading to deeper hardwood forest, and is frequently lined with deep green clumps of Christmas fern, which add their color to the forest year-round.

A pleasant shorter hike that goes between the golf course and the lodge is the Indian Bluff Trail. It will take you past sandstone bluffs that formed shelters for the local American Indians. But do not get your hopes up about the Indian Window found along this trail. Described in the park's literature as "the only natural arch within the park," it should be renamed the Indian Keyhole—you will miss it if you blink.

If you exhaust all the hiking possibilities within the park, you can strike off from the Indian Bluff Trail onto the 13.5-mile Pennyrile Nature Trail, which will take you out of the park and into the state forest. It will tax your joints but reward you with several scenic overlooks along more sandstone bluffs.

FACILITY DETAILS

Lodge: The stone and wood Pennyrile Lodge, containing just 24 guest rooms, resembles an overgrown cottage. Spring through fall, colorful flowerbeds decorate the exterior. The side away from the entrance is landscaped with low stone walls and patios, bird feeders, more flowerbeds, and benches where you can relax and watch the boats on the lake. All the rooms have patios or balconies, too. In winter, you can sit in front of the fireplace in the lobby, which has a peaked ceiling supported by dark wood beams. The lodge also has a recreation room, a gift shop, and the 200-seat Clifty Creek Restaurant. The dining room overlooks the lake.

The charming stone lodge at Pennyrile Forest State Resort Park.

WESTERN

A family takes in the view of the lake at Pennyrile Forest State Resort Park.

Cottages: There are 12 cottages, with either one or two bedrooms. Four are tucked into the woods east of the lodge. Eight are located along the lake and have their own docks. The best one may be the Honeymoon Cottage, number 508. It has a sleeping loft containing a double bed that you get to by climbing a spiral staircase. A window at the head of the bed looks out into the hillside. It is like sleeping in a tree house for grownups.

Campground: The park has a 68-site campground located in woodlands and well away from the park's entrance on Kentucky 109. All sites have utilities hookups. The park's miniature golf course is at the edge of the area, and there is also a playground. You can walk along a park road for easy access to trails that lead to the boat dock, beach, or lodge.

Trails: This is definitely a walker's park. The nine trails vary in length from 0.2 mile to 4.5 miles and all intersect, so you can cover most of the park on foot. Some feature stone steps and wooden shelters constructed by Works Progress Administration workers in the 1930s, during the restoration of Pennyrile State Forest. (The current park opened in 1954.) The WPA built the dam that impounded the lake, too, and old millstones from the site are imbedded in the wall of the dam, which you can see from the Clifty Creek Trail.

American lotus blooms by the lake in August.

Fishing and Boating: Choose a small boat or fish off the dock near the beach. The lake is stocked with largemouth bass, bluegill, crappie, and channel catfish, among others.

Swimming: The swimming pool by the lodge and the sandy beach by the boat dock are open from Memorial Day to Labor Day. The beach is sheltered in a small cove and separated from the lake by a stand of another plant that is rare in Kentucky, the American lotus (*Nelumbo lutea*). The plate-shaped leaves, between one and two feet across, hover above the surface of the water, supported on slender stems. During July and August, the large, yellow lotus blossoms break through the blanket of green.

Golf Course: The course has 18 holes and is situated along a small valley in the park. It is surrounded on either side by woods, and a creek flows through the middle of it. Golfers will have one kind of water challenge or another on each hole of the front 9.

Other Recreation: Tennis courts, basketball courts, picnic shelters, miniature golf course, playground, paddleboats in season. The park has a full-time recreation director who plans activities ranging from rook card game tournaments to games for children. There is a full-time naturalist, too.

Special Events: Adventure Pennyrile Forest naturalist-guided hikes (March, April, September), Fishing Derby (June), Western Weekend country dancing (September), Geocaching Weekend (October).

MORE TO EXPLORE

Pioneers made a medicinal tea using the leaves of the pennyroyal plant. It was used to treat a variety of maladies including colds, fevers, indigestion, and kidney and liver disorders. Oil from the plant was also used as insect repellent. However, do not try any of this. *The Peterson Field Guide to Medicinal Plants and Herbs of Eastern and Central North America* by Steven Foster and James A. Duke gives the following warning:

> Pulegone, the active insect repellent compound in essential oil, is absorbed through the skin and converted into a dangerous liver cancer–inducing compound. Ingesting essential oil can be lethal; contact with essential oil can cause dermatitis. Components of essential oil may be particularly dangerous to epileptics.

WICKLIFFE MOUNDS
STATE HISTORIC SITE

94 Green Street
Wickliffe, KY 42087
(270) 335-3681
http://www.parks.ky.gov/findparks/histparks/wm/
26 acres

J UST OVER a thousand years ago, Pope Urban II launched the Crusades, the Chinese were manufacturing gunpowder, and Macbeth was the king of Scotland. In short, the medieval world was a turbulent place.

On the other side of the globe, at the confluence of the Ohio and Mississippi rivers, life was much more peaceful. It was here, for 250 years (from about 1100 to 1350), that a community of Mississippian mound builders thrived. They were here and then they were gone, and no one knows what happened to them. But the excavations at Wickcliffe Mounds State Historic Site provide a comprehensive picture of their lives.

Knowledge of this village emerged when an amateur archaeologist, Colonel Fain W. King, purchased the land in 1932 and started digging. He opened up the site as a tourist attraction called the Ancient Buried City.

Implements in the lifeways building give insight into daily life nearly 1,000 years ago at Wickliffe Mounds State Historic Site.

WESTERN

From 1984 to 2004, the site was owned by Murray State University, and further research was conducted. In 2004, Wickcliffe Mounds joined the state parks system.

Thanks to the efforts of the archaeologists, you can walk into three of the mounds, which are protected by Quonset-style structures. It is better to visit on a cool day, since they are not air- conditioned and can be sweltering inside.

The lifeways building has excavations of the villagers' homes. Among the many artifacts are pottery vessels and cooking tools. The people here did not just fashion utilitarian objects; they had fun with them. Many are made in whimsical animal shapes, especially birds.

Those are not real skeletons in the cemetery building. They are plastic replicas, but they do show how carefully and respectfully the Mississippians honored their dead. Forensic study of the actual remains yielded information on life expectancy, some of the diseases the people had (arthritis, for example), and facts about the food they ate. Several detailed panels in this building catalog this information.

Actual remains have been replaced with plastic skeletons, which illustrate the care and respect with which the American Indians buried their dead.

WESTERN

The Mississippians favored wattle-and-daub construction. In the architecture building, you can see how this intricate method, involving interweaving flexible lengths of wood and plastering it with mud, was done. Because this mound contains only one residence, it is thought to have been the village chief's home.

A fourth mound on the site is not covered by a hut. It is the ceremonial mound you can see looming near the west side of the parking lot when you arrive. The important communal building of the village sat atop this mound, and if trees had been cleared away, there would have been a view of the river.

After spending all the time you want studying the contents of the mounds, you may want to stretch your legs on the short Woods Walk Trail, which makes a 200-yard loop through the trees behind the cemetery building.

FACILITY DETAILS

Museum and Gift Shop: You enter the site through a welcome center. There is an admission charge. View the excellent orientation film, which explains the history of the site. There is much more information in the museum displays here, too. The gift shop carries some replicas of Mississippian pottery, among other items.

Special Events: Hands-on workshops featuring various American Indian crafts, including pottery-making and bead crafts, are held throughout the year.

MORE TO EXPLORE

The park is about 30 miles west of Paducah, a city named after Chickasaw chief Padouca, who, unlike the Mississippians, apparently never existed. But you will see his statue downtown at the corner of 19th and Jefferson streets, a triumph of art over evidence. The city is home to the Museum of the American Quilter's Society, the largest quilt museum in the world. In addition to traditional, antique quilts, the displays include striking modern examples of the quilter's craft. My personal favorite honors the Beatles, complete with a quilted Yellow Submarine. The museum is well worth a visit. For more information, go to http://www.quiltmuseum.org/.

WESTERN

ADDITIONAL
PARKS

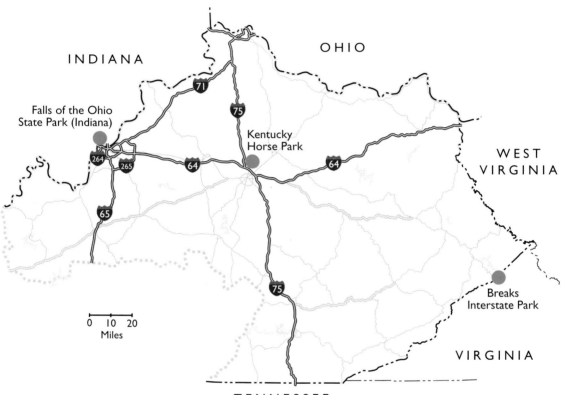

INDIANA

OHIO

Falls of the Ohio
State Park (Indiana)

Kentucky
Horse Park

WEST
VIRGINIA

Breaks
Interstate Park

VIRGINIA

0 10 20
Miles

TENNESSEE

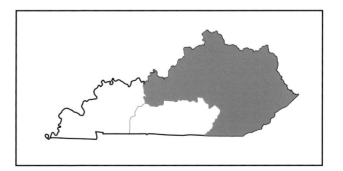

ADDITIONAL PARKS

• Year-round
○ Seasonal

ADDITIONAL PARKS		Park Acres	Lake Acres	Lodge and Dining Room	Cottages	Campground	✈:Airport; ▲:Air Camp
Breaks Interstate	Elkhorn City	4,600	12	○	•	•	
Falls of the Ohio	Clarksville	1,404					
Kentucky Horse Park	Lexington	1,224				○	

Golf (18-Hole, 9-Hole, or D: Disc Course)	Marina (L: Boat Launch Only)	Rental Boats	Swimming (P: Outdoor Pool, I: Indoor Pool, S: Slide, B: Beach)	Trails (Miles)	Riding Stables (○: Equestrian Trails)	Mountain Biking	Tennis Courts	Miniature Golf	Playgrounds	Picnic Area	Museum or Nature Center	Recreation/Interpretation Program
	L	○	P	15+	○/○					•		
	L								•	•	•	
			P							•	•	

BREAKS INTERSTATE PARK

Kentucky/Virginia Highway 80
Breaks, VA 24607
(276) 865-4413 or (800) 982-5122
http://www.breakspark.com/
4,600 acres; 12 lake acres

The view from the Tower Overlook shows where the Russell Fork of the Big Sandy River carves out the Grand Canyon of the South.

VISITORS TO BREAKS INTERSTATE PARK will find beautiful hiking trails bisecting rugged terrain across Kentucky and Virginia, an abundance of native flora and fauna, a wonderful legend about buried treasure, and one of the most notable geological features in the United States.

That feature is the canyon from which the park (and the region) takes its nickname. The Russell Fork of the Big Sandy River has carved a five-mile-long, 1,600-foot-deep gorge, the oxbow of which is located in the park. It is the largest canyon east of the Mississippi River, hence the Breaks' designation as the Grand Canyon of the South.

Unlike the western gash in the earth, the Breaks is covered in dense forest made up of more than 60 species of trees. These make the park a fine

destination for fall foliage viewing. In spring and summer, the trails are great for wildflower spotting, and you will be treated to a variety of delicate fungi and ferns, too. Flower species include showy orchis (*Orchis spectabilis*), cardinal flower (*Lobelia cardinalis*), herb robert (*Geranium robertianium*), and wood lily (*Lilium philadelphicum*).

The woods are home to more than 100 kinds of songbirds, and you may very well see golden eagles riding the thermals above the canyon. Stay alert for glimpses of secretive animals when you are walking here. My one brief peek at a bobcat came on a visit to the Breaks.

There are several different overlooks at which you can stand to look down at the river or across the canyon to the water-ringed mountain formation called the Towers. It looms large in the Breaks treasure legend.

The story goes that in the 1760s, John Swift, a former English sea captain, abandoned his

Whitewater kayaking and rafting on El Horrendo rapids, a portion of the Russell Fork of the Big Sandy River.

Sourwood shows its fall color on the cliff of the Clinchfield Overlook.

naval career and became a trader among the American Indians of Virginia. He ventured into Kentucky, where he allegedly came across a vein of silver, established a mining operation, and minted a fortune's worth of silver coins. Swift had to travel back and forth to the mines, bringing supplies from and taking coins to Virginia. When American Indian hostilities broke out on one such trip, he supposedly hid a treasure in silver somewhere on the Towers. Shawnees frequently sheltered in the caves that pockmark the area.

Before he could recover the treasure, the Revolutionary War broke out, and Swift was arrested and imprisoned by the British, who were annoyed at their former military man's sympathy for the colonists. When he was finally released, he was blind and in terrible health. Swift was never able to find his hidden silver. To this day, neither has anyone else. There is a very good reason for this. The credibility of Swift's story is strained by the fact that geologists have never been able to locate even a molecule of silver in the area.

FACILITY DETAILS

Lodges: There are two. The contemporary, glass-walled Rhododendron Lodge has the restaurant, gift shop, and meetings facilities, as well as rooms overlooking the canyon. The views from the Breaks Motor Lodge are a little more obscured by trees, and the rooms are darker inside. The park is open year-round, but the lodges and restaurant are open only from April 1 to mid-December.

Cottages: Woodland cottages are open year-round and are rented for a minimum of two nights. One- and two-bedroom sizes are available. Two-story cottages have the living space and kitchen on the ground floor and beds and bathrooms upstairs.

Campground: A road running north off the lake road leads to three separate camping areas, which have a total of 122 sites. All have utilities hookups. Reservations are not taken.

Visitor Center: Exhibits and displays here focus on the history, geology, flora, and fauna of the park. Coal mining is important in the region, and an exhibit about the formation and extraction of coal is excellent. Another economic aspect examined is corn, including its fermentation for use in moonshine. Photographs illustrate the history and development of the park. The center has public restrooms.

Trails: The park has more than 15 miles of hiking trails. Several are quite short and lead from parking areas to canyon overlooks. Expect to climb lots of steps. Many of the overlooks are linked by the Overlook Trail, but caution is advised because there are few railings. Maps with trail descriptions are available at the visitor center. Booklets are available describing the features of the Ridge Trail and Geological Trail. A very pretty trail in June and July, when the rhododendron is blooming, is the Laurel Branch

Catawba rhododendron blooms along the Laurel Branch Trail at Breaks Interstate Park.

Trail. The woods it passes through are dominated by hemlocks and mixed hardwoods. Backcountry overnight camping is permitted on longer trails, but you must register at the visitor center.

Whitewater Rafting: Available in October on certain weekends when water is released into Russell Fork River from the reservoir. The class IV–VI rapids are for experienced rafters only.

Swimming: The park's Olympic-size pool is located at one end of the lake. Open seasonally.

Fishing and Boating: The pocket-size Laurel Lake is stocked with bass and bluegill. You can rent a pedal boat in which to tool around the lake or fish from one if you like.

Other Recreation: Occasional weekend concerts are held in a small amphitheater. There are a stable and riding trails. Golfing packages are available for overnight guests at the park to play golf on the nine-hole course at the nearby Willowbrook Country Club.

MORE TO EXPLORE

The Pine Mountain Trail, some of which is already open, will eventually be 120 miles long and stretch from Breaks Interstate Park along the crest of Pine Mountain to Cumberland Gap National Park. Trail guides, maps, and more information are available at http://www.pinemountaintrail.com/.

ADDITIONAL

FALLS OF THE OHIO STATE PARK

201 Riverside Drive
Clarksville, IN 47129
(812) 208-9970
http://www.fallsoftheohio.org/
1,404 acres

FIVE MINUTES' WALK down a sandy, winding path leads to the edge of a vast inland sea, teeming with more than 600 species of corals, shellfish, trilobites, sponges, sea snails, crinoids, and fish. But this ocean, washed over by the freshwater of the Ohio River, is frozen in rock. And it covers more than 220 acres of Devonian limestone, the largest such exposed formation in the world. The chance to view this fossilized sea life dating from nearly 400 million years ago is just one of several reasons to visit Falls of the Ohio State Park.

The park is located only minutes across the Clark Memorial Bridge from downtown Louisville. Visitors can walk out and over this paleontological treasure and have a very strong sense of being by the seashore. Not only are mineralized shells and corals so numerous that it is impossible not to step on them, the cadence of rushing water over and around the nearby dam regulating the river level masks nearly all other sounds, except, heard here hundreds of miles from the nearest modern ocean, the cries of seagulls.

A fossil of a giant snail is embedded in the Devonian limestone.

Gulls and other species of shorebirds, including herons, egrets, osprey, and even, very occasionally, white pelicans, are found here because of the unique habitat.

The so-called falls are actually a series of rock shelves located at a bend in the river. Shallow pools form in depressions in the rock, trapping fish, which birds hunt. The wooded shoreline of the park contains cottonwoods, sycamores, and other hardwoods, providing perches and nesting sites. So binoculars, as well as waterproof hiking boots, are recommended. Birders have recorded 265 species at the park.

The birds are not the only two-footed anglers here. The currents near the park are popular with humans, too. People brandishing poles from aluminum rowboats or along the shoreline regularly land trophy-size catfish. They are only 1 of 125 species of fish found here, including paddlefish and gar, descendants of swimmers who lived during the age of the dinosaurs, a period much more recent than that of the fossils in the limestone.

Even though this is an Indiana state park, it is included in this book because the site has a prominent place in Kentucky history. Ever visible from the fossil beds and only a couple of miles away is the skyline of Louisville. The city is here because the 2 miles of rapids at the falls were the only nonnavigable portion of the Ohio River between its origin, near Pittsburgh, and where it joins the Mississippi, 980 miles downstream.

In 1778, George Rogers Clark led a band of soldiers and others down the Ohio. They were forced to stop at the falls and thus established a settlement. It eventually grew into the city of Louisville, named in honor of the French king, Louis XVI, who aided the Americans in their fight for independence from the British.

For Clark's success in capturing the Northwest Territory from the redcoats, the fledgling American government awarded him and his soldiers a land grant along the Ohio River in 1783. Clark built a cabin overlooking the falls on seven acres that soon became known as Clark's Point. A replica of the cabin can be found on the site today, within the park and accessible from a trail through the woods.

Famed artist and ornithologist John James Audubon, who lived in Louisville from 1808 to 1810, visited Clark at his retreat. Audubon was much taken with the bird life at the falls and wrote about it extensively in his journals, including about the snowy owl, a northern species that can be seen here in the winter.

A statue at the entrance to Falls of the Ohio State Park commemorates two other visitors to the Revolutionary War general. It shows the general's

Canoes are recommended transport for watching birds and exploring fossil beds at Falls of the Ohio State Park.

younger brother, William Clark, and Meriwether Lewis clasping hands. The famous pair who lead the Corps of Discovery expedition to the Pacific and back first met here in 1803.

FACILITY DETAILS

Museum: Details of the biology and history of the Falls of the Ohio are presented in a 16,000-square-foot interpretive center, the striking exterior of which is built of layers of different kinds of stone, mimicking geological strata. The museum features exhibits about the ancient sea life and about prehistoric and colonial-era American Indians at the falls, as well as aquari-

ADDITIONAL

ums containing both coral reef and Ohio River fauna. For the best fossil viewing, visit in late summer and early fall, when the river level is down. Note that collecting is not permitted. Birding is rewarding all year round.

Special Events: Young Paleontologists Camp (June), Sun Circle Native American Celebration (June), Fossil Festival (September), Raptor Day (October).

MORE TO EXPLORE

For more information about the geology and history of the park, read James E. Conkin and Barbara M. Conkin's *Handbook of Strata and Fossils at the Falls of the Ohio* (University of Louisville Studies in Paleontology and Stratigraphy) and George Yater's *Two Hundred Years at the Falls of the Ohio: A History of Louisville and Jefferson County* (Filson Historical Society).

KENTUCKY HORSE PARK

4089 Iron Works Parkway
Lexington, KY 40511
(859) 233-4303 or (800) 678-8813
http://www.kyhorsepark.com/
1,224 acres

WELCOME TO THE WORLD of everything horse. If you are the parent of a horse-mad daughter and bring her here, she will be completely smitten. And since it is usually, though no longer exclusively, boys who become jockeys, sons will not be immune either.

Appropriately located in the heart of the largest concentration of horse farms in the world, Kentucky Horse Park is not devoted only to the racing and hunting Thoroughbreds. Fifty or so breeds of horses, from tiny dwarf ponies to massive draft horses, live here. In the summer, there is a daily parade of breeds, a live show of the park residents. Riders have costumes appropriate to the horse's or pony's geographic origins (Arabian, Spanish, Plains Indians, and more). The Wild West Show entertains visitors, as well.

A resident greets a visitor.

Bronze sculpture by John Claggett of eventing champion Bruce Davidson, Sr. on his Irish Sport Horse, *Eagle Lion*.

But you can do more than watch the horses here. You can ride with them and meet and greet a few.

Horse-drawn trolleys take visitors on tours around the park. If you want to saddle up, there are guided rides, and there is no need to be an expert equestrian. Some illustrious retired racehorses call the park their home, including the famous Cigar.

Anyone who has ever ridden a horse, especially at a canter or a gallop, knows why the winged Pegasus is such a persistent mythic figure. Riding a horse is the closest you can get to flying without leaving the ground, at least for more than a few inches. The park has a nifty exhibit laid out on the sidewalk near the life-size bronze statue and gravesite of the mighty Man o' War. Lines mark the stride lengths of famous horses. It is an exercise in awestruck appreciation to try to jump from one stride marker to the next.

In addition to exhibiting horses, the park hosts scores of national and international events each year from cross-country to polo. The most prestigious annual competition is the Rolex Kentucky Three-Day Event, one of the qualifying events for the American equestrian Olympic team.

In 2010 the World Equestrian Games will be held at Kentucky Horse Park. Consisting of world championships in eight sports for horses and riders, this is the first time that the international competition will be held outside Europe.

ADDITIONAL

Sunset at Kentucky Horse Park.

FACILITY DETAILS

Hours: Open daily mid-March to October 31. Open Wednesday through Sunday from November 1 to mid-March. Closed the day before Thanksgiving and Thanksgiving Day, Christmas Eve and Christmas Day, and New Year's Eve and New Year's Day.

Campground: There are 260 paved sites with utilities hookups. Primitive camping is also an option. The grounds include a swimming pool, store, service building with showers and laundry facilities, and games courts. Open seasonally.

Museums: The International Museum of the Horse is devoted to 50 million years of horse evolution and association with humans. You will encounter prehistoric eohippus and armoured steeds with knights on board, as well as racing trophies, horse-drawn vehicles, and tack collections. The American

Saddlebred Museum is devoted to the first breed of horse developed in Kentucky. The Saddlebreds are the elegant animals ridden in dressage rings.

Art Gallery: Travelling exhibits of equine paintings, drawings, and sculptures from all over the world rotate through the gallery. There is an annual juried exhibit and sale in the fall by the American Academy of Equine Art.

Gift Shop: Everything from horse key chains and jewelry to books and hand-painted furniture is included in the extensive stock. Proceeds benefit the park.

Special Events: Rolex Three-Day Event (May), Southern Lights Holiday Festival (November–December), numerous competitive equestrian events and shows throughout the year.

Grazing in a paddock.

Displays at the Southern Lights Holiday Festival.

MORE TO EXPLORE

Midway, located equidistant between Lexington and Frankfort, originated as a railroad town. Today, its Main Street is distinguished by an active railroad track running down the center, with 19th-century storefronts on either side housing antiques stores, boutiques, and bistros. Only a 15-minute drive from the Kentucky Horse Park, Midway is a great place to either unwind after a park visit or have lunch before you go. The town is also home to Midway College, an all-women's school that offers a variety of degrees including equine studies. If your horse-mad daughter is thinking about turning her obsession into a career, you might make a college visit while in Midway. Information about the community, its businesses, and the college can be found at http://www.midwayky.net.

ADDITIONAL

ACKNOWLEDGMENTS

PAM SPAULDING AND I spent a fascinating year traveling Kentucky to research and photograph this book. We could not have done so without the help of many people.

Karen Miller was marketing director for the Kentucky state parks when we started work on the project, and she was our invaluable travel agent. She arranged for our overnight accommodation in park lodges and cottages.

Former commissioner of state parks J. T. Miller, former deputy commissioner John Kington, Commissioner Gerry van der Meer, and Deputy Commissioner Larry Totter have all been very supportive, as has Marcheta Sparrow, secretary of the Kentucky Tourism, Arts and Heritage Cabinet. Gil Lawson, the cabinet's communications director, arranged all of our meetings with these officials and helped fill in the blanks of parks details.

Staff members of the parks were unflagging in their cooperation, giving us guided tours and "insider information" before turning us loose to explore on our own. Thanks go to Monica Conrad (Barren River), Stefanie Gaither and Paul Tierney (Blue Licks Battlefield), Greta Reynolds and Sue Thomas (Buckhorn), Coy Ainsley and John Jordan (Carter Caves), Cindy Lynch (Columbus-Belmont), Dollie Cruse (Green River), Claire Earnhart and Paul Verespy (Greenbo), Ty Lindon (Jenny Wiley), Paula Sherman (Lake Malone), Alice Heaton (My Old Kentucky Home), Chad Green (Perryville Battlefield), Ron Bryant (Waveland), Kathleen White (White Hall), Carla Hildebrand (Wickliffe Mounds), and Jack Bailey (William Whitley House).

Carey Tichenor, director of the Division of Recreation and Interpretation in the Department of Parks, also helped with information. Joyce Bender of the Kentucky State Nature Preserves Commission provided details about state nature preserves within the state parks.

Martin Childers, executive director of the Jenny Wiley Theatre, gave Pam permission to photograph during a performance. William Jones, proprietor of Jonesie's Overland Stagecoach in Bardstown, provided the coach and horses in the exterior photograph of My Old Kentucky Home.

Thanks also go to Joanna Goldstein, who was both Pam's voice-activated mobile light stand and her all-around camera equipment schlepper. Bill and Susan Schuetze joined us at Kenlake, where Bill provided guidance about the blues and Susan catered our picnic lunch. Susan also shared her golf knowledge with me.

My former neighbor Nancy Shives looked after Mac, E.T., Froggy, and Shadow and substituted in the occasional Indiana University Southeast class while I was traveling the state. Once I was home in Louisville, many meals caught on the fly while writing were provided by my brother, Hunter Reigler, who imported barbecue mutton from Owensboro, and by my neighbor Jackie Atchison, who left red beans and rice on my doorstep.

Pam and I also need to thank two people we have never met. The many, many hours driving to parks passed much more quickly because we listened to the audio versions of several Harry Potter books. Thank you for writing them, J. K. Rowling, and thanks for reading them to us, Jim Dale.

Finally, thanks to all the people associated with the University Press of Kentucky, including director Stephen Wrinn; director of editing, design and production Melinda Wirkus; and copy editor Anna Laura Bennett. We thank acquisitions editor Laura Sutton most of all for coming to us with the idea to write and photograph a new book about the Kentucky state parks.

ABOUT THE AUTHOR AND PHOTOGRAPHER

SUSAN REIGLER was, from 1992 to 2006, the *Louisville Courier-Journal*'s restaurant critic and also regularly wrote travel and science articles. From 2006 to 2007, she was the newspaper's first full-time staff travel writer. She is the author of *Kentucky,* a volume in the Fodor's Compass American Guides series, first published in 2001 (2nd ed., 2006), and *Adventures in Dining: Kentucky Bourbon Country* (2005). Many of the articles she wrote about Kentucky state parks for the *Courier-Journal* travel section were also published in the *Indianapolis Star, Cincinnati Enquirer,* and *Nashville Tennessean.* Reigler has degrees in zoology from the University of Oxford and in music from Indiana University. She writes and teaches in Louisville.

PAM SPAULDING joined the photography staff of the *Courier-Journal* in 1972. Spaulding's work has been published in many calendars and books, as well as in magazines such as *Horticulture, National Geographic,* and *Traveler.* She is a graduate of Ohio State University and was a Nieman Fellow at Harvard University.